The Napoleonic Wars

An Enthralling Guide to Global Conflict, Revolutionary Tactics, and the Empire's Expansion

© Copyright 2024 - All rights reserved.

The content contained within this book may not be reproduced, duplicated, or transmitted without direct written permission from the author or the publisher.

Under no circumstances will any blame or legal responsibility be held against the publisher, or author, for any damages, reparation, or monetary loss due to the information contained within this book, either directly or indirectly.

Legal Notice:

This book is copyright protected. It is only for personal use. You cannot amend, distribute, sell, use, quote, or paraphrase any part, or the content within this book, without the consent of the author or publisher.

Disclaimer Notice:

Please note the information contained within this document is for educational and entertainment purposes only. All effort has been executed to present accurate, up-to-date, reliable, and complete information. No warranties of any kind are declared or implied. Readers acknowledge that the author is not engaging in the rendering of legal, financial, medical, or professional advice. The content within this book has been derived from various sources. Please consult a licensed professional before attempting any techniques outlined in this book.

By reading this document, the reader agrees that under no circumstances is the author responsible for any losses, direct or indirect, that are incurred as a result of the use of the information contained within this document, including, but not limited to, errors, omissions, or inaccuracies.

Free limited time bonus

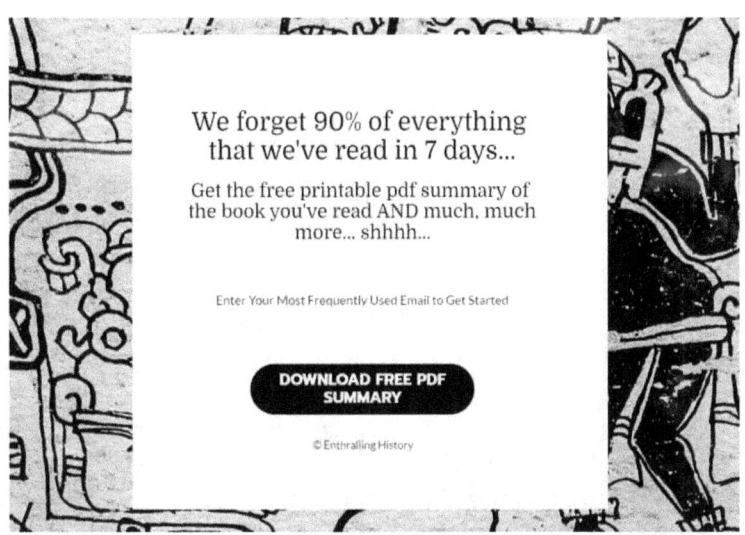

Stop for a moment. We have a free bonus set up for you. The problem is this: we forget 90% of everything that we read after 7 days. Crazy fact, right? Here's the solution: we've created a printable, 1-page pdf summary for this book that you're reading now. All you have to do to get your free pdf summary is to go to the following website: https://livetolearn.lpages.co/enthrallinghistory/

Or, Scan the QR code!

Once you do, it will be intuitive. Enjoy, and thank you!

Table of Contents

INTRODUCTION 1
CHAPTER 1: THE RISE OF NAPOLEON 3
CHAPTER 2: THE REFORMATION OF FRANCE..13
CHAPTER 3: REVOLUTIONARY BATTLEFIELD TACTICS AND WARFARE..22
CHAPTER 4: NAPOLEON'S CONTINENTAL WARS BEGIN 32
CHAPTER 5: THE BATTLE OF TRAFALGAR: NAPOLEON'S DEFEAT AT SEA...43
CHAPTER 6: NAPOLEON'S ZENITH 52
CHAPTER 7: THE PENINSULAR WAR: NAPOLEON'S STRUGGLE IN SPAIN AND PORTUGAL 62
CHAPTER 8: THE CULTURE OF THE TIME...72
CHAPTER 9: THE INVASION OF RUSSIA: NAPOLEON'S CATASTROPHIC CAMPAIGN 82
CHAPTER 10: THE WAR OF THE SIXTH COALITION AND THE ABDICATION...94
CHAPTER 11: THE HUNDRED DAYS AND WATERLOO: NAPOLEON'S LAST STAND..104
CONCLUSION 114
HERE'S ANOTHER BOOK BY ENTHRALLING HISTORY THAT YOU MIGHT LIKE...117
FREE LIMITED TIME BONUS..118
BIBLIOGRAPHY 119
IMAGE SOURCES 127

Introduction

The Napoleonic Wars were an important moment in European history and Western civilization. They are a major part of the saga of a military genius named Napoleon Bonaparte. Napoleon ranks with the great masters of military science, and his tactics are still studied in military institutions and universities worldwide. He was more than just a military genius, though. Napoleon was also a lawgiver and a champion of ideas that would transform Western civilization. The Napoleonic Code remains one of the primary legal texts of history, ranking with the Code of Justinian as a powerful instrument of social change. However, what we remember most about Napoleon are not his innovations in law but rather his wars.

The opening years of the 19th century in Europe can best be described as campaign season for the French army. Napoleon was constantly at war with other powers in Europe. His amazing understanding of military science permitted him to outmaneuver armies that were much larger than his time and time again. The French emperor could innovate and adapt quickly. He recognized the need to combine surprise with speed and decisive action to outmaneuver his opponents. Napoleon built a formidable military machine that struck fear in his enemies while also gaining respect at the same time. The Grande Armée was his creation and the driving force behind his outstanding military achievements.

Napoleon was a champion on the battlefield, but he was also successful at the negotiating table. He was able to forge alliances and reach agreements with others. Napoleon also had a unique capability of manipulating Continental politics to be successful.

Napoleon Bonaparte believed that fate and luck were his constant companions. However, that was not always the case. The Peninsular Wars and the Russian campaign of 1812 proved that this man was mortal and did not always make the best decisions. Moreover, his enemies learned from their defeats. This became evident at the Battle of Leipzig (also known as the Battle of the Nations), where the Little Corporal was no longer the master of the fight. He would ultimately lose all he had won, but the path he blazed until the final engagement at Waterloo is still seen as brilliant.

The Napoleonic Wars are an amazing story of the rise and fall of one man. The analysis of these years show us where he made brilliant decisions, how he arrived at them, and what caused him to make mistakes that eventually proved disastrous.

The wars were not spontaneous but resulted from what happened in France in the late 18th century. The Napoleonic Wars followed eleven years of conflicts that pitted Revolutionary France against other European nations. We will briefly examine the French Revolution to see how it influenced the later years of the wars.

Simply put, the Napoleonic Wars testify to the immense genius of Napoleon Bonaparte. The battles he fought and the accomplishments he achieved are worth every minute we take to study them. We will explore these in this work, and we hope readers will benefit from learning about the man and the period in which he lived.

Chapter 1: The Rise of Napoleon

<u>The Lad from Corsica</u>

Napoleon Bonaparte was born in the city of Ajaccio on the island of Corsica on August 15th, 1769. He was the son of Carlo Buonaparte and his wife, Letizia. The boy was part of a large family of minor Corsican aristocrats. At one time, Corsica was the possession of Genoa, but France acquired it the year before Napoleon was born. Napoleon grew up learning French, and he became increasingly acquainted with the new owner of his homeland.

Napoleon was sent to France to receive an education when he was nine. He studied at the Royal Military School in Brienne and then the École Militaire in Paris. He excelled at mathematics and history, but the young man stood out in military subjects. Napoleon had a keen intellect and intensely studied warfare tactics, the construction of fortifications, and military history. His understanding of complex concepts was remarkable for a young man his age.

His years at the École Militaire would be time very well spent. Napoleon learned more about cavalry tactics and artillery at this institution, and he graduated a second lieutenant of an artillery regiment when he was only sixteen years old.[1]

---

[1] Editors, H. (2023, April 24). Napoleon Bonaparte. Retrieved from History.com: https://www.history.com/topics/european-history/napoleon.

If history didn't play out the way it did, Napoleon could have been a second lieutenant for a long time. One's family was more important in military advancement than actual talent. A young man could become an officer on the staff of a general based on family connections or a good word from an influential friend. It was also possible to purchase a military rank if an individual had the right amount of money. It would have been difficult for Napoleon to rise through the ranks in this system. There was a genuine chance this ambitious young man could have spent his military career posted to a garrison in some remote and forgettable part of France. Fortunately for him, Napoleon entered the military at the right time.

The Three Estates of France

France was in turmoil before Napoleon gained power. The French Revolution kickstarted events that resulted in Europe being at war for over twenty years.

France had a class system that was centuries old. The First Estate was at the top of the pyramid and consisted of the Catholic clergy. (Protestantism was severely repressed by the revocation of the Edict of Nantes in 1685.) Approximately 10 percent of French land was owned by the Roman Catholic Church and was tax-exempt.

The Second Estate comprised the French aristocracy. They were the powerful elite of France and controlled positions of authority in the military and the government. There was a division within the Second Estate. "Nobles of the sword" were those whose titles had been in their families for generations. They had been granted their status for military service or from favors given by the king. "Nobles of the robe" were aristocrats who achieved their status by being administrators, financiers, or judiciary officials.

The last estate, the Third Estate, included more than just the peasantry. It consisted of the commoners, including artisans, farmers, merchants, and anyone who was not part of the nobility or clergy. More than 90 percent of the French population was part of the Third Estate. It was the largest group in French society, and it was the most oppressed.

A medieval adage declared, "The priests pray for all, the lords fight for all, and the peasants pay for all." That was true a thousand years later. The clergy were exempt from taxes. The aristocracy was required to pay poll taxes and the *vingtième* (one-twentieth of annual income, or 5 percent). Neither estate was asked to pay the direct tax, the *taille*. The

Third Estate had to pay that and other taxes and levies on their income and holdings.[2]

The class structure in France created considerable social tension. The Third Estate rightly saw that they were required to carry the country's burden, and yet the other two estates did not have to pay heavy taxes even though they typically earned more money than them.

Moreover, there were certain privileges that the aristocracy enjoyed that they had maintained for centuries. They were not about to give them up. Some severe problems within the French government aggravated the animosity between the Third Estate and the First and Second Estates.

The Debt Crisis

France was involved in several major wars during the 18th century and had to recover from the Mississippi Bubble, a speculation frenzy that destroyed many people's fortunes. By the 1780s, however, the most significant problem that France was experiencing was a debt crisis brought on by helping a friend.

France became a significant ally of the Americans during the American Revolutionary War, and it was probably because of French aid that the Americans even succeeded. That assistance cost a considerable amount of money. It is estimated that France spent approximately 1.3 billion livres on the war, which added to the already existing national debt. When the war ended, France was left with a debt of over 3.3 billion livres.

This debt had to be repaid by direct and indirect taxes levied on the French people. The tax collection system in France during Louis XVI's reign was inefficient. Royal tax officials collected direct taxes, but indirect taxes were farmed out to the ferme générale ("general farm") and its subsidiary, the régie générale.

The tax system complicated French tax collection. The ferme générale tax collectors were given significant authority to collect taxes and seize property if necessary. They had special privileges and legal protection. They also became incredibly wealthy because they were often corrupt.[3]

---

[2] Mark, H. W. (2022, March 7). The Three Estates of Pre-Revolutionary France. Retrieved from World History Encyclopedia: https://www.worldhistory.org/article/1960/the-three-estates-of-pre-revolutionary-france/.

[3] Emerson Kent.com. (2024, May 25). Taxation in Pre-Revolutionary France. Retrieved from

The tax system was not meeting the needs of the national budget. Debt service was the largest part of the government expenditures, and by 1780, paying off the debt amounted to 43 percent of national expenses.

Louis XVI was not blind to the problem. He knew that it had to be resolved. He appointed Charles Alexandre de Calonne to be the controller-general of French finances in 1783 and asked him to look at the situation and come up with an answer to the problem. De Calonne found a system that was in complete chaos. He audited the nation's accounts and records and scrutinized how the money was managed. His final recommendation was to tax the country across the board. This meant that those exempted from taxes or who paid very little would lose their privileges. Louis XVI was confronted with telling the aristocracy they had to pay their fair share. He did not want to do it, but the problem would not go away.

Portrait of Charles Alexandre de Calonne'.

Emersonkent.com:
http://www.emersonkent.com/history_dictionary/taxation_in_pre_revolutionary_france.htm

Additionally, getting loans to cover the debt from European banks was not an option. France was a bad credit risk. Bankers understood how much financial trouble France was in and hesitated to provide funds.[4]

The problems became worse as the 1780s progressed. Finally, in 1788, the crisis came to a head. There was a bad harvest, and the state was not able to collect the money necessary to pay all the bills. The treasury was bare, and the only way to correct matters was to call the Estates General and ask that parliamentary body to come up with a solution to allow France to make ends meet.

The Military of the 1780s

The French military faced difficulties that undermined its effectiveness as a fighting force. The debt crisis cut into military appropriations, depriving all branches of the funds necessary to be a major military presence. Lack of funds meant there was not always enough money for training or replenishing military equipment. The nobility controlled the upper ranks of officers, and soldiers from the middle and working classes resented the lack of an equal chance to advance.

Soldiers and sailors became dissatisfied with the status quo. While they were loyal to the monarchy, they wanted better opportunities for advancement, and the customs of the Ancien Régime were blocking their path to achieve something greater. The French Revolution promised changes, and many in uniform would take advantage of the new, more egalitarian regime.

The Road Leads to War

The French Revolution went from a spark to a bonfire quickly. Traditions, privileges, and laws that had existed for centuries were wiped out in months. France's social and political landscape was radically changed.

The European ruling class was very concerned. It was one thing to be an enlightened despot; a constitutional monarch was something else. That meant sharing power, and the monarchs did not want that at all. They kept a worried eye on what was happening in France as news of the

---

[4] Sparknotes.com. (2024, May 25). The French Revolution (1789-1799). Retrieved from Sparknotes.com: https://www.sparknotes.com/history/european/frenchrev/section1/.

liberal changes spread.

The tension building up between Revolutionary France and the royal crowns of Europe finally broke. The French Legislative Assembly declared war on Austria on April 20th, 1792. An allied army of Austrians and Prussians moved into France to restore the Bourbon monarchy, and a French army was sent to stop the allied force. The two armies would meet at Valmy on September 20th. The allies had a combined force of approximately eighty-four thousand men, and they opposed a French contingent under François Christophe de Kellermann, who had forty-seven thousand troops.

Before the first cannons were fired, it appeared this would be a lopsided victory for the allies. After all, the duke of Brunswick was one of the best commanders of Europe, and he had a nearly two-to-one advantage in troops over Kellermann. Surprisingly, though, the French won. A revolutionary army of volunteers defeated a highly professional opponent. The immediate result of the battle was the abolition of the French monarchy and the creation of the first French Republic on September 22nd.[5]

The Battle of Valmy, painted by Horace Vernet.[a]

How was that possible? The French had been significantly outnumbered. It was more than courage that won the day. The French

---

[5] Hickman, K. (2019, September 4). French Revolutionary Wars: Battle of Valmy. Retrieved from ThoughtCo.: https://www.thoughtco.com/french-revolution-battle-of-valmy-2361106.

army that took the field in 1792 was transformed from the royal regiments of 1788. There was a great upswelling of patriotism in France and revolutionary zeal brought on by symbolic gestures, such as the composition of songs like "La Marseillaise."

A Titanic Change

The French Revolution convinced many aristocratic officers to leave France. Their departure created vacancies in the officer ranks, which were quickly filled by energetic men who had talent. The changes in command were extensive. Although 90 percent of the officers before the French Revolution were from the aristocracy, only around 3 percent of those nobles were still in the army in 1794.

The French army was reorganized. There were three distinct army units: Army of the Center, Army of the North, and Army of the Rhine. France also changed the way men were called up for service. Instead of having local levies of troops, Revolutionary France employed *levée en masse*, which was a total mobilization of the population. Conscription generated massive military forces that increased the size of the French army.

Tactics also changed. The French began to use light infantry tactics that prioritized mobility. Light infantry was used more often, and skirmishers were frequently used to start engagements. The army as a whole concentrated on offensive strategies in which they took the fight to the enemy rather than sit back and wait for the enemy to come to them.[6]

An advantage the French Revolutionary Army had was its artillery. Horse artillery was first used at the Battle of Jemappes on November 6th, 1792. Although the equipment and caliber of the cannon were standard for the day, the artillerymen's esprit de corps and efficiency permitted the weapons to be fully utilized.[7]

The French became proficient in siege warfare. Encirclement and scorched earth tactics enabled them to be highly successful in siege campaigns. By using cannons and mortars, the French were able to blast holes through enemy fortifications, allowing infantry units to pour

---

[6] Jensen, N. D. (2024, May 25). Organization of French Revolutionary Armies 1791-1801. Retrieved from French Empire.net: https://www.frenchempire.net/articles/armies/.

[7] Williamson, M. (2016, August 5). French Napoleonic Artillery in Action. Retrieved from Weapons and Warfare: https://weaponsandwarfare.com/2016/08/06/french-napoleonic-artillery-in-action/.

through the gaps caused by the cannonballs and shot.

Engineers were important in the French Revolutionary Army. They ensured French soldiers were well protected in the field with fascines (bundles of brushwood used for protection) and could advance across rivers on quickly constructed bridges.

Lazare Carnot helped to reform the French military during these years. He had the organizational skills to turn the French army into a highly professional fighting force. Carnot instituted the *levée en masse* and merged newly conscripted troops with veterans, allowing the newcomers to learn combat skills rapidly. His efforts gave him the moniker Organisateur de la Victoire ("Organizer of Victory").[8]

The Top of the Class

The military reforms of the French Revolution unlocked a treasure trove of geniuses. The French officer corps was now defined by talent, not titles. Men rose in prominence in the ranks due to their ability to think on their feet and audaciously lead. Napoleon Bonaparte was in a class of very ambitious, highly intelligent young officers. He would rise to the top of the class by the end of the century. Part of his success was admittedly from being in the right place at the right time, but there was more to this young Corsican than just good luck. Napoleon had qualities and skills that made him great.

Initial Success

Toulon was an important French naval base on the Mediterranean coast. Royalist sympathizers had control of the city and turned the port over to an Anglo-Spanish fleet after the British commander, Vice Admiral Lord Hood, agreed to hold the city on behalf of the imprisoned child king, Louis XVII (Louis XVI was executed on January 21st, 1793). It was essential for the revolutionaries to retake the city, and on August 28th, 1793, Toulon was placed under siege by the French government.

Napoleon was given command of the besieging army's artillery after the original commander was wounded. The young captain made the most of his new assignment and conceived a plan to retake Toulon from the allies. The French attacked the forts surrounding the city on December 16th, 1793. They retook the defenses. The Anglo-Spanish

---

[8] Napoleonguide.com. (2024, May 25). Lazare Carnot. Retrieved from Napoleonguide.com: https://www.napoleonguide.com/carnot.htm.

forces were forced to leave Toulon, which the French officially retook on December 19th. Napoleon received credit for the victory and was promoted to brigadier general several days after the battle. It was the beginning of a series of successes for Napoleon.

Command of the Army of Italy

Napoleon's next major assignment would be the artillery commander of the Army of Italy. He would assume command of the entire Army of Italy on March 27th, 1796.

The Italian campaign that followed showcased Napoleon Bonaparte's brilliance. He took command of a demoralized army and turned it into a significant fighting force. The young general (he was only twenty-five years old!) used the cavalry, infantry, and artillery efficiently and made mobility, speed, and aggressive tactics priorities. His victories ultimately led to the Treaty of Campo Formio of 1797, which forced Austria to give up northern Italy to France.

Analysis of Napoleon's Achievement

The Italian campaign proved Napoleon's ability as a commander. The Army of Italy was a demoralized unit, and his leadership skills turned things around quickly. Napoleon had something that other generals did not have: charisma. He motivated his men with messages highlighting the honor, rewards, and glory that would come with victories. The commanding general also shared his troops' hardships and endured the same conditions the ordinary private had to suffer.

Napoleon was also brave. He led troops across a bridge at the Battle of Lodi (May 10th, 1796) despite withstanding fire from the enemy. He made decisions quickly and changed course if the circumstances required it. His ability to lead troops in combat conditions was exemplified at the Battle of Montenotte (April 12th, 1796). There, he split his forces and beat two opposing armies.

Bonaparte became the man of the hour in Revolutionary France. He was a general who delivered impressive victories and kept the French Republic safe from its enemies. The Egyptian campaign (1798-1801) was a serious risk, but it allowed Napoleon to use one of his military innovations to win an important victory.

The Battle of the Pyramids (July 21st, 1798) was a major confrontation between Napoleon and the Mamluk rulers of Egypt. He introduced the divisional square in that engagement. The design was straightforward: a division with three brigades was formed into three separate squares. The infantry was on the outside, the cavalry was on the inside, and the artillery was at the corners. There was nothing novel about squares; armies had long used them for defense against cavalry. However, Napoleon used the divisional square as an offensive weapon. The Mamluk army was massacred.

Napoleon was politically savvy. His understanding of the political environment made him capable of making cold-blooded decisions. He ordered French artillery to open fire on a mob of French civilians in the street battle of 13 Vendeemiaire (October 5th, 1795). Several hundred people were killed, but Napoleon's order saved the French government from dissolving.

Charles Monnet's depiction of Napoleon's opening fire on civilians.[iii]

However, his loyalty to his troops did not mean he was willing to die with them. Napoleon eventually abandoned his soldiers in Egypt and returned to France to achieve personal political objectives. Both events suggest the man was not above playing politics if it served his purposes.

The end of the 18th century saw France become a republic. It had successfully beaten its military adversaries and was a force to be reckoned with in Europe. The French Revolutionary principles of liberty, equality, and fraternity captured the imagination of people across Europe.

Tensions were growing between the social classes. People were daring to demand rights they once thought they would never have, and tempers were rising. The ruling elite needed to do something to stop the radical ideas from growing; otherwise, they might suffer the same fate as Louis XVI.

Chapter 2: The Reformation of France

The French Revolution brought enormous change to France, but there was still more work to do. Reforms were still required to end practices that had been accepted for centuries without question. France was a major laboratory of political and social improvements, and the reformation efforts continued from the 18th century to the 19th century. Napoleon would be a catalyst for these changes.

The Napoleonic Code: The Beginning

Napoleon became the first consul of France in 1800. He successfully maneuvered his way through the politics and intrigue of the later days of the French Republic and overthrew the Directory with the Coup of 18 Brumaire on November 9th, 1799. He was a very influential person despite his age (he was only thirty-one). He set for himself a task that, when it was completed, would affect France over two hundred years later. This was the Napoleonic Code.

The Napoleonic Code was an ambitious project, and France desperately needed it for several reasons:

- To end the legal confusion.

    France did not have a single code of law, and statutes could vary from one region to another. The Napoleonic Code would create a system of laws that could be applied uniformly across France.

- To enhance a central government.

  A standardized legal code would permit a stronger central government that could curtail regional powers held by the local judiciary.

- To encourage a more robust economy.

  Contract and property law are the basis for a strong economy. There are, of course, other rules of commerce that need to be followed as well. All of this would be part of the Napoleonic Code. In addition, foreign investors would feel more comfortable putting their money into French enterprises if they knew that the economy was stable and following set rules of conduct.

- To codify the French Revolution.

  The French Revolution changed the country, and the reforms needed to be consolidated. The Napoleonic Code would carve these changes into the fabric of French society.

The Process of Codification

An attempt to codify French law was initiated as early as 1790, but the code drafts of 1793, 1794, and 1796 were all rejected. A commission was established in December 1799, and Jean-Ignace Jacqueminot provided an outline that was rejected. Napoleon decided that once and for all, there would be a code for French law. He would use his power and influence as first consul to complete the project.

A final commission was created in 1800. It was chaired by Jean-Jacques-Régis de Cambaceeres, Second Consul of France. The work on the draft of the code was completed in 1801, and it was finally published on March 21st, 1804. Its original title was "Civil Code of the French," and it would be renamed the Napoleonic Code in 1807.[9]

The Parts of the Code

The Napoleonic Code's framework was influenced by an earlier codification of law, the Code of Justinian. The French version distributed French law into four sections:

---

[9] DetailedPedia.com. (2024, May 26). Napoleonic Code. Retrieved from DetailedPedia.com: https://www.detailedpedia.com/wiki-Napoleonic_Code.

1. Persons

2. Property

3. Acquisition of Property

4. Civil Procedure (This would be placed in a separate code in 1806.)[10]

The principles of the Napoleonic Code were impressive and novel for its time. Here are a few examples of what it introduced:

- All male citizens were equal before the law. Privilege based on aristocratic titles was abolished.
- Public institutions were no longer under the control of ecclesiastical authorities.
- People could enter freely into contracts, given certain limitations.
- Criminal law was strictly defined, and rules were established for civil litigation. A person was presumed innocent until proven guilty.
- Property rights were protected.[11]

The immediate impact of the Napoleonic Code on French society was clarity. Instead of a witch's brew of edicts and sometimes contradictory laws, France now had a code that could be followed anywhere in the country. The rules specified in the Napoleonic Code were in clear language that anyone could understand.

Religious dissent was tolerated under the code. This was a significant change. France had been torn apart by religious wars in the 16th century, and there were still problems of religious oppression of non-Catholics. The Napoleonic Code ended that. Freedom of religion was the accepted law of the land. Protestants and other non-Catholic groups were safe.

Of course, there were parts of the Napoleonic Code that modern society would find unacceptable. Men had greater control over their families, and women were still subordinate. Men had equal rights under the law, but these rights were not extended to women. Slavery in the colonies had been abolished during the French Revolution, but the code

---

[10] DetailedPedia.com. Napoleonic Code.

[11] Britannica, E. o. (2024, May 18). Napoleonic Code. Retrieved from Britannica.com: https://www.britannica.com/topic/Napoleonic-Code.

reinstated it.

The Lasting Legacy

The Napoleonic Code was the legal template that European and Latin American nations copied during the 19th century, particularly by those countries that had been occupied by the French during the Napoleonic Wars. The Napoleonic Code is still the basis for the legal systems of many modern nations.

There is one interesting fact about the Napoleonic Code. The United States legal system is founded primarily on English common law with one exception. The Napoleonic Code still influences Louisiana, which was once a French possession. There is a difference in the legal standards of practice for lawyers in Louisiana as opposed to the rest of the United States. For instance, in Louisiana, laws like community property and forced heirship dictate that property acquired during marriage is jointly owned and that a portion of a deceased person's estate must go to their children. In other states, property distribution and inheritance can be more flexible and determined through wills.[12]

Napoleon's reform was made against the backdrop of the French Revolution. Radicals wanted a significant transformation of society and were not concerned about the cost. Napoleon was more pragmatic.

He recognized that French society was essentially a center-right culture. Radicals could propose social changes of tidal-wave proportions in Paris that would not take in Lyons or Provence. The French Revolution was extremely violent, and its accomplishments were bathed in French blood. Napoleon accepted the boundaries within which he could make needed reforms and avoided going too far. To him, the Reign of Terror would remain a unique historical moment and nothing more.

Concordat of 1801

The greatest fracture in French society during the French Revolution was the split between the secular government and the Roman Catholic Church. The French Revolution caused the deaths of thousands of clergy and the loss of church property. The radicals tried to make France

---

[12] DailyHistory.org. (2024, May 26). Why Has the French Civil Code Had a Lasting Influence on Contemporary European Law. Retrieved from DailyHistory.org:
https://www.dailyhistory.org/Why_has_the_French_Civil_Code_had_a_lasting_influence_on_contemporary_European_law.

as atheist as possible, but there were still millions of French who yearned for a reconciliation with the church. This was not a call for a return to superstition. The church had been an integral part of the social structure for thousands of communities, and it was sorely missed.

Additionally, a lack of reconciliation meant a large group of Catholics could become serious opponents of the government, which Napoleon did not want. The opportunity for an understanding between the Roman Catholic Church and the state came about thanks to the election of a new pope.

Barnaba Niccolò Chiaramonti was elected pope on March 14th, 1800, and took the papal name of Pius VII. The new pope wanted to return the faithful in France to the church, and Napoleon was tired of religious conflict in his country. The two men commenced serious negotiations in November 1800.[13]

Napoleon entered into the discussions with three objectives: the renunciation of former church property by the Roman Catholic Church, the reinstitution of the church in France with new rules for appointing bishops, and the payment of the clergy's salaries by the state. Pius VII wanted Catholicism to be the official religion of France once again. Of course, it wouldn't be that simple. There would be much back and forth on these points and others.

Fortunately, the pope was willing to be flexible and make significant concessions. His primary concern was to enable Catholics to freely practice their faith in the open and for priests to be able to do their duties unmolested. Pius wanted to ensure the church's future and allow its followers to worship peacefully. In return, Napoleon's secular power in France would be recognized.

The Final Terms

The talks were very constructive since both sides were hoping for an amicable resolution to the dispute. An agreement was finally reached, and the Concordat of 1801 was signed on July 15th, 1801. The following is what they agreed on:

---

[13] Coppa, F. J. (2018, May 18). Concordat of 1801. Retrieved from Encyclopedia.com: https://www.encyclopedia.com/philosophy-and-religion/christianity/roman-catholic-and-orthodox-churches-councils-and-treaties/concordat-1801.

- The Roman Catholic Church was recognized as the religion of the majority of the French citizens. This did not mean that Catholicism was the state religion, but it did concede that most French were practicing Catholics.
- The French government would appoint Catholic bishops, who would then be consecrated by the pope.
- The property lost during the French Revolution was irretrievable; the Roman Catholic Church would not regain possession of any of it, but the state would pay salaries to the clergy.
- The church was allowed to train priests in seminaries and hold public worship. Those who went to Mass could do so freely and without fear of oppression.

The radicals in France who were in favor of a robust secular government criticized the Concordat of 1801 as a betrayal of revolutionary principles. At the same time, French royalists protested the resulting centralization of power within France. Napoleon ignored the protests, and Pius VII quietly accepted the concessions. What was important was that an agreement had been reached between the government and the most powerful social force in France. Devout Catholics were now free to practice their faith and be loyal citizens as well. There would be no Catholic fifth column behind Napoleon's back in the years to come.[14]

The Concordat of 1801 was a sensible balance between a secular state and a religious institution. It was a pragmatic answer to a nagging problem and stabilized French society. The raw emotions of the French Revolution were starting to calm down as church and state were able to agree to disagree and still respect the position of each other.

Economic Changes

Napoleon had other interests he wanted to address that would create a stable French economy. France spent years operating with a financial system that was woefully inefficient, and Napoleon was committed to ending that state of affairs.

He also had a political agenda. The existing financial chaos in France had private financial institutions competing with regional banks.

---

[14] A fifth column is a group of people who undermine a larger group or the nation.

Napoleon wanted greater economic efficiency, and a central bank fit into his overall policy of centralization. His idea would be similar to the British Bank of England but would include achieving national economic and private commercial objectives.

Private capital was used to found the Bank of France, but state funds were also used. The Bank of France (Banque de France) would have a close connection with the French government, and the state appointed the governor and the two deputy governors of this financial institution. The Bank of France was permitted certain privileges. Most importantly, it was allowed the exclusive right to issue banknotes in Paris for fifteen years. The Bank of France's power to issue banknotes would later be extended to the entire country of France.[15]

The Bank of France was able to stabilize the national currency and ultimately standardize the currency in France. Public debt is always a concern for a central bank, and the Bank of France consolidated French public obligations. It allowed international and domestic confidence in France's stability to increase, and the country was able to secure loans with fewer problems than before. The restoration of confidence in French currency and its ability to manage public debt generated considerable prosperity for France in the early 19th century.

The Bank of France played a significant role in the years immediately following its creation. It supported the Napoleonic Wars by extending needed credit and financing military expenditures. Napoleon was later able to wage wars knowing there would be monetary backing for his efforts.

The Lycées

Napoleon's wish to centralize and standardize France also extended to education. Earlier attempts to do that during the French Revolution were not successful, but Napoleon's efforts produced positive results. A central point of his educational reforms was the lycées.

The lycées were secondary schools, and their task was to educate future administrators, professionals, and military officers in France. Beforehand, education was centered primarily on developing the aristocracy. The lycées were boarding schools that accepted students on scholarships and also paying boarders and day students. The curriculum

---

[15] Britannica, T. E. (2024, May 24). Banque de France. Retrieved from Britannica.com: https://www.britannica.com/money/Banque-de-France.

was centered on a humanistic model of education, but it also had courses in science, mathematics, history, geography, and literature, among other areas of study. It was a broad education that would produce a well-rounded graduate.[16]

The lycées were not established just for the sake of educating young minds. The curriculum was intended to promote critical thinking, problem-solving skills, and the intellectual capabilities that military officers needed. Successful graduates would be able to transition into French military academies without a problem and pursue further military education.

Napoleon's changes also included some very useful projects for both the economy and society at large. These included infrastructure, such as better roads, improvement of the ports, and canal work. These all contributed to the growing prosperity of a country that had been wracked by ten years of revolutionary change. All of this benefited France and made Napoleon extremely popular.

Everything Napoleon accomplished, which he did in just a few years, would become a model for others to follow in the years to come. Like the United States Constitution, the Napoleonic Code would be emulated and improved upon. The Concordat of 1801 gave nations ideas on how to manage the sometimes-tricky relationship between church and state. The critical thinking and problem-solving encouraged by the lycées are used today by highly successful educational systems worldwide.[17]

However, there was another side to all this activity. Napoleon centralized France and established standards that would do more than make the nation an economic power. France was capable of financing and conducting military campaigns that might include absorbing territories beyond its borders. Revolutionary ideals were put in their proper place, but they were not entirely forgotten. The French had the means beyond fiery rhetoric to make substantial changes in Europe.

Rulers of other countries became more concerned about what was going on in France and the possibility of these very liberal ideals coming

---

[16] Savoie, P. (2024, May 26). Lycée. Retrieved from Faqs.org: http://www.faqs.org/childhood/Ke-Me/Lyc-e.html.

[17] Globallytaught.com. (2024, May 26). Education Systems Around the World: A Look at 4 Top School Systems. Retrieved from Globallytaught.com: https://globallytaught.com/blog/education-systems-around-the-world/.

across the French borders. Napoleon needed to be checked, if not stopped entirely. But that was not going to be easy. Napoleon Bonaparte was a phenomenon many had never seen before. If any foreign government underestimated this man, they would find out in a few years just how wrong they were to do so. Napoleon was establishing a modern society in France, but he was also creating a massive military machine that was nearly unstoppable.

Chapter 3: Revolutionary Battlefield Tactics and Warfare

Military reform and innovation were ongoing in France. The reforms made to the ranks of the French Revolution continued into the 19th century. Napoleon fanned the flames of change, and the French military became the most formidable army in Europe as a result.

Nathan Bedford Forrest, a Confederate general during the US Civil War, once made an astute observation describing how an army can succeed on the battlefield: get first with the most. It means that a successful military force must be able to move quickly and deliver maximum force at the right moment. Napoleon understood this concept long before General Forrest was even born.

Napoleon changed the structure of the French army in 1800. He organized the army into corps or corps d'armée. These military units were larger than divisions and were able to operate independently of the main force.

The corps was a small army. It had its own cavalry, infantry, and artillery. The corps was intended to be able to operate by itself, and Napoleon would often have the corps separated from each other by a short distance. They could come together in major battles or be used to fight the enemy on several fronts, which could effectively outmaneuver a larger force. Separate corps could also come to the aid of another corps since they were ordinarily positioned no more than a two days' march from each other.[18]

Napoleon is credited with coining the phrase that an army marches on its stomach. That is true, but it is also correct to say that a long supply train can slow down an army during a march. Napoleon instructed his corps commanders to live off the land as much as possible. In other words, the French military was expected to collect the food and provisions they needed from local areas as they marched through them. This posed a hardship for the civilians living in the area, but it also meant that the army was not slowed down by a cumbersome supply train, nor did it rely on supply depots.

The enhanced mobility of the French army was noticeable in the field. Bonaparte could order forced marches in which his army could cover as much as thirty miles in one day. This speed allowed him to take advantage of any opponent who was trying to collect its forces or regroup. The best example of French speed and mobility happened in the Battle of Ulm. Napoleon was able to quickly surround his enemy and force them to surrender.[19]

Artillery and Cavalry

Both artillery and cavalry were essential to the success of the French. Napoleon emphasized mobility by using lightweight cannons. This enabled the artillery to be brought up quickly and used with devastating effect on an opposing army that was still trying to position its heavier guns. A special group of soldiers known as voltigeurs was organized to support the artillery.

The cavalry units were more than just advanced scouts for the Grand Armée. Napoleon used them as shock troops and employed massive cavalry charges to break the enemy lines and create the chaos necessary to turn the tide of battle in France's favor. The cuirassiers (cavalrymen equipped with a sword, pistols, and a cuirass, a type of armor) were ordered to charge at top speed and demoralize the enemy.

---

[18] Wesson, M. J. (2024, May 28). The Development of the Corps d'armée and Its Impact on Napoleonic Warfare. Retrieved from The Napoleon Series: https://www.napoleon-series.org/military-info/organization/c_armycorps.html.

[19] Mark, H. W. (2023, July 10). Ulm Campaign. Retrieved from World History Encyclopedia: https://www.worldhistory.org/article/2249/ulm-campaign/.

An illustration of cuirassiers.[iv]

The cavalry was made even more intimidating by the use of horse artillery. These were cannons that could be moved by horse-drawn teams quickly across the battlefield. They added significantly to the power of the French army.

Psychological Warfare

Sun Tzu, the famous Chinese general and strategist, wrote that the most significant battle is not physical but psychological and that the war is waged in the mind.[20] We do not know if Napoleon read the works of this ancient military strategist, but the French commander certainly used psychological warfare to his advantage.

Napoleon employed propaganda to intimidate his opponents and used disinformation campaigns to make it appear that victory was inevitable and that no one could beat the French army. He controlled the narrative better than his enemies.

---

[20] Powerplace.org. (2023, July 28). Top 51 Timeless Sun Tzu Quotes: Mastering Strategy and Leadership. Retrieved from Powerplace.org: https://powerplace.org/blogs/quotes/mastering-strategy-and-leadership-unveiling-51-timeless-sun-tzu-quotes.

The famous painting of Napoleon crossing the Alps is overly romanticized to make Napoleon appear larger than life.

His battle tactics were often intended to confuse. He feigned a retreat to lure the enemy into traps, and surprise attacks were coordinated to catch opposing armies off guard. Napoleon encouraged personal myths about his invincibility. He wanted to be viewed as unstoppable by his foes and make them doubt their ability to beat him. He was often successful on this front.

The Marshals of France

The French field marshals in the Napoleonic Wars were a stellar group; the closest in quality to them would likely be the German field marshals of the Wehrmacht in World War II. Some of these men had been with Napoleon since the Italian campaign; they hitched themselves to Napoleon's star and were richly rewarded. Historians debate on who was the best of the best in this class. We propose that the following men stand out the most. In order to avoid showing preference, we will discuss them in alphabetical order.

- Louis-Alexandre Berthier

    Louis-Alexandre Berthier did not command massive cavalry charges, but he was a very important player in the Napoleonic Wars. He was Napoleon's chief of staff for almost twenty years and was involved in nearly every major campaign. Berthier managed all logistics and planning for Napoleon's military ventures. He had remarkable administrative skills, and his loyalty to the emperor was unquestioned. He could take Napoleon's notions and turn them into easily understood orders.

    Berthier shined in the Ulm campaign, where his organization of Napoleon's instructions resulted in a total defeat of the Austrian army. However, Berthier was not in favor of gradually stretching the communication lines in the Russian campaign, which restricted the French army's ability to maintain a supply line during the harsh winter of 1812.[21]

- Jean-Baptiste Bernadotte

    Bernadotte was both a skillful administrator and an excellent field commander. He had a unique ability to move through the territory of Napoleonic politics and balance that successfully with military affairs. Bernadotte played a tactical role in the Battle of Austerlitz, which was Napoleon's most significant victory. His efforts at the Battle of Jena were not as impressive, and he was criticized for being unable to sufficiently engage the troops under his command.

    What made Bernadotte stand out was his final opposition to Napoleon. He was elected to be the successor to the king of Sweden on August 20th, 1810, and he formally became king of

---

[21] Napoleon.org. (2024, May 28). Louis-Alexandre Berthier. Retrieved from Napoleon.org: https://www.napoleon.org/en/history-of-the-two-empires/biographies/berthier-louis-alexandre/.

Sweden as Charles XIV John in 1818. The French occupation of Swedish Pomerania in 1812 and problems with the Continental System caused Bernadotte to switch sides and join the European alliance against Napoleon in 1813.[22]

- Jean Lannes

    Personal bravery and almost reckless courage distinguished Lannes from the other marshals on this list. He was a commander who was not afraid to lead from the front, which constantly exposed him to danger. Lannes could assess the situation quickly and make informed decisions at the right moment. He was one of the marshals who had been with Napoleon throughout his career.

    Lannes commanded the left wing of the French army at Austerlitz. He successfully held off Russian assaults, which permitted Napoleon to move over the Pratzen Heights at a strategic moment. Lannes continued to be one of the most dependable field commanders in the Grande Armée and assisted competently in the Spanish campaign.

    He died on May 31st, 1809, from wounds suffered at the Battle of Aspern-Essling. Napoleon was overcome with grief when he heard of the loss of his close friend. In a letter to Lannes's widow, he wrote, "I lose the most distinguished general of my armies, my companion arms for 16 years, and whom I consider my best friend."[23]

- Michel Ney

    Napoleon referred to Michel Ney as the bravest of the brave. He was another field marshal who was willing to lead from the front. Despite his rank, Ney was devoted to his soldiers. He was deeply concerned for their welfare.

---

[22] Hickman, K. (2020, January 2). Napoleonic Wars: Marshall Jean-Baptiste Bernadotte. Retrieved from ThoughtCo.com: https://www.thoughtco.com/napoleonic-wars-marshal-jean-baptiste-bernadotte-2360137.

[23] Green, J. (2004, April). Napoleon Bonaparte's "Roland": Marshal Jean Lannes. Retrieved from Warfarehistorynetwork.com: https://warfarehistorynetwork.com/article/napoleon-bonapartes-roland-marshal-jean-lannes/.

Ney's finest hour would happen during Napoleon's greatest disaster. Ney was placed in command of the rearguard during Napoleon's retreat from Moscow. According to legend, he was the last Frenchman to leave Russia, guarding the retreating troops until the last man crossed the border.[24]

Ney pledged allegiance to the restored Bourbon dynasty after Napoleon abdicated. However, he changed sides when Napoleon came back to France from his exile in Elba. Ney fought hard at the Battle of Waterloo, but his desperate cavalry charge, which did not have infantry support, was the final straw in the French defeat. Ney would later be executed for treason by the Bourbons because he returned to Napoleon's side.

- Joachim Murat

Murat was a flamboyant showman and an aggressive field commander. He was always stylishly dressed and stood out from the more conservatively dressed commanders. He also became Napoleon's brother-in-law.

What made Murat noteworthy was his ability to lead the cavalry. He could move quickly and lead cavalry assaults that made a difference in numerous battles. His attacks against

A portrait of Joachim Murat.[24]

the allied forces at Austerlitz were instrumental in sealing the final victory. Unfortunately for the field marshal, his brilliance on the battlefield was not matched by his political decisions. He became the king of Naples in 1808 and lost his throne in 1815. While trying to regain his throne, Murat was captured by the new king of Naples and died before a firing squad.

---

[24] Green, J. (2002, April). Michel Ney's Retreat. Retrieved from Warfarenetwork.com: https://warfarehistorynetwork.com/article/michel-neys-retreat/.

An interesting feature of Napoleon's marshals is that they performed brilliantly under his command, but when they were given independent commands, these field marshals were not as good. It was Napoleon's ability to lead and inspire that enabled these men to be heroes. Without the emperor, they were not particularly stellar.

European nations worried about the revolutionary ideas coming out of France. Greater attention should have been paid to how France was centralizing itself and, even more importantly, what changes were happening in the French military. In a few short years, France transformed from a traditional army to one full of new technologies and superior strategic thinking. It could take on one enemy or an alliance of foes and have a good chance of winning. Here are some comparisons between France and its major potential enemies: Austria, Great Britain, Prussia, and Russia.

Austria

The French army was comprised primarily of native-born Frenchmen. Every soldier spoke the same language and shared the same cultural heritage. That unity was helpful on the battlefield since orders did not need to be interpreted.

The Austrian army was a diverse mixture of Germans, Flemings, Walloons, and Italians. The military units were consequently split into various ethnicities. The most immediate problem was that a diverse army spoke several different languages, requiring delays in interpreting commands. The quality of the soldiers varied from one nationality to another.

The Austrian army was a professional unit with an excellent heavy cavalry. However, the military tactics of the Austrian army were more conservative than the French. Battlefield flexibility was not a feature of the Austrian forces. There would be dramatic reforms to the Austrian army after the defeat at Austerlitz, but the French had an overall superior quality at the start of the Napoleonic Wars.

Great Britain

The British had overwhelming naval superiority. It proved its ability against the French at the Battle of the Nile and the Battle of Trafalgar. The French navy could not compete with its rival.

At the beginning of the 19th century, the British army was a small but well-disciplined force. It would not engage with the French until the Peninsular War, and its leadership would change dramatically when the duke of Wellington was in charge. Napoleon had plans to invade Great Britain, but the British fleet prevented that.

Prussia

In 1804, the Prussian army was living with a reputation it had won decades earlier. The army had been unstoppable under the command by Frederick the Great, but it had not improved in the years since the king's death. The army was well disciplined, but its military strategy was weak compared to Napoleon's. Prussian tactics were rigid and not effective.

Prussia would pay dearly for not modernizing its military. The French rolled over the Prussians in several battles, notably at Jena. After France soundly beat the Prussians, military reforms were introduced that permitted Prussia to return to its former military greatness.

Russia

Russia participated in the Wars of the Second, Third, and Fourth Coalitions, but then moved to the sidelines until it was invaded in 1812. It was not a modern army when the Napoleonic Wars started.

The regiment was the largest unit in the Russian army. Soldiers were recruited from the peasantry and were roughly treated by officers. Officers were recruited from the aristocracy, which was the general practice of European armies in the 18th century. Their training was not very good.

Russian soldiers were brave and could endure severe hardships, but the army as a whole was lacking. It would take the severe defeat at Austerlitz for Russia to take the necessary steps to modernize its military.[25]

An overall assessment concludes that the French were more than a match for any or all of its enemies on the battlefield. French military innovations under Napoleon made the Grande Armée the best fighting force in Europe.

There was one final advantage the French had over their enemies. The French army was used to winning. Since Valmy, French troops had been on the battlefield with only a few short truces between active engagements. The French did lose a few battles, but they won even

---

[25] Napoleonistyka.atspace.com. (2024, May 28). Russian Army of the Napoleonic Wars. Retrieved from Napoleonistyka.atspace.com: Napoleonistyka.atspace.com.

more. They were accustomed to being the victors on the battlefield under the direction of Napoleon.

French soldiers were confident of their success, which gave them greater morale than their opponents. The French were often outnumbered in the battles, but they were certainly not outfought. In addition, the French faced enemy troops that had to travel hundreds of miles to reach a common rendezvous point. The French corps moved close to each other and could quickly come together as a result. French soldiers fought under a uniform strategy; allied armies with different tactical maneuvers had to learn how to fight as a single force.

The French military's overall superiority would become evident in the next few years, much to the regret of the enemy.

Chapter 4: Napoleon's Continental Wars Begin

The Roman Republic existed for hundreds of years. It fell apart when the pressure became too much and tore at the social fabric. The empire ceased to exist when a charismatic leader with an army at his back walked onto the stage. The same happened to the French Republic.

The French Republic spent years trying to be a cohesive entity. However, the National Assembly gave way to the Reign of Terror, which then gave way to the Directory. Napoleon captured the imagination of the French people and led an army that adored him. He was declared counsel for life, but it gradually became apparent that he was more than just a representative of the people. Ultimately, the powers that be in France recognized reality, and Napoleon was crowned emperor of France. The French Republic was officially dead.

The First Consul

All of that didn't happen overnight, though. Napoleon seized control of the French government in the Coup of 18 Brumaire and created the French Consulate, of which he was the first consul.[26]

At the time, France was fighting a war with the Second Coalition. This war saw France pitted against an alliance of Austria, Great Britain,

---

[26] Anne S. K. Brown Military Collection. (2024, June 4). Napoleonic Satires. Retrieved from library.brown.edu: https://library.brown.edu/cds/napoleon/time2.html

Russia, the Ottoman Empire, Portugal, and Naples. The allies could not communicate properly amongst themselves, and Napoleon took advantage of their confusion. He took his army across the Alps in May 1800 and defeated the Austrians in the Battle of Marengo on June 14th, 1800. Austria was ultimately forced to sue for peace and signed the Treaty of Lunéville on February 9th, 1801, which took Austria out of the war. Great Britain and other allies continued to fight until the British signed the Treaty of Amiens on March 25th, 1802, which led to the war's end.

France was at peace, and Napoleon had the ability to push through some of the reforms he wanted. He did not accept criticism well and did not appreciate any opposition. He declared himself the first consul for life in August 1802, but he wanted more than that. Napoleon drafted a new constitution that included succession if he should have a son, and it was increasingly clear that the type of government Napoleon wanted was not revolutionary but more authoritarian. What he really desired was a crown on his head.

The Empire of France

French military success and the treaties that confirmed their conquests dramatically enlarged France. France came to include Belgium, Luxembourg, Piedmont, Genoa, and the Duchy of Parma. German territory on the left bank of the Rhine was also under French control. And these are just the territorial gains. Napoleon created client states, which included the Batavia Republic, the Italian Republic (later the Kingdom of Italy), and a reconfiguration of the Swiss Confederation.

In Italy, Napoleon dissolved the Republic of Venice in 1797 and made dramatic changes to the political map of Italy. The Cisalpine Republic was created in 1797 from a union of northern Italian states. He carved the Ligurian Republic out of what was once Genoa. The Roman Republic would come into being after the Papal States were invaded, but that political entity did not last long. The Parthenopean Republic was formed in southern Italy, but it also collapsed. Finally, the Cisalpine Republic was incorporated into the Italian Republic. The Kingdom of Italy would later absorb most of these entities, but the political boundaries that had endured for centuries in Italy were gone because of Napoleon.[27]

---

[27] Marino Berengo, C. M. (2024, June 4). Italy-The Napoleonic Empire 1804-14. Retrieved from

The changes in Germany were more dramatic. Before Napoleon, Germany had been a hodgepodge of principalities, ecclesiastical states, and imperial cities. Many of these political entities were absorbed into larger ones, such as Bavaria, Baden, and Württemberg. Those states were given extra territory as a reward for being reliable French allies. They continued to be part of the French sphere of influence and provided necessary troops for Napoleon's later campaigns.

The First French Empire at its peak in 1812.[vii]

The reorganization included the introduction of the social and legal reforms instituted by the French Revolution and Napoleon himself. The traditional way of governance and doing things was destroyed in a matter of a few years. Europe had not seen anything comparable to what Napoleon did since the Reformation.

Britannica.com: https://www.britannica.com/place/Italy/The-acquisition-of-Venetia-and-Rome.

Vive l'Empereur!

Napoleon was crowned emperor of France on December 2nd, 1804. It would be easy to say that personal vanity and ambition motivated Napoleon to want the imperial crown, but there was more to it than that. Personal advancement was just one of his motivations.

France was militarily successful, but its government was in shambles. The Directory was corrupt and inefficient. Order and stability were necessary for France to thrive. Napoleon was able to stabilize the government as first consul, and he wanted to continue making changes that he felt would make France better.

It is essential to remember that Napoleon Bonaparte was a true agent of change. The Concordat of 1801 and the Napoleonic Code are examples of his wish to improve French society. Additionally, he believed that he was a protector of the revolutionary ideals that had gripped France. He wanted to be able to spread those principles. The imperial title would permit him to introduce reforms into societies weighed down by antiquated traditions and privileges. However, he also wanted a dynasty, and he wanted to have the glory that came with being emperor. Nevertheless, he would use that position to bring about social change.[28]

Napoleon made one significant move before the Napoleonic Wars began. He sold Louisiana, a vast territory in the North American continent, to the newly founded United States. There is much discussion of how the Louisiana Purchase benefited the United States and gave the country valuable resources. The sale benefited France as well.

A decision had to be made on where France would concentrate its interests. Louisiana was an immense territory, but it would have to be defended. The British were on the northern border, in Canada, and could invade the French territory. All the British needed to do was take New Orleans; the rest of the land would then be more of a burden than a blessing.

Napoleon learned from the French setbacks in the Haitian Revolution, in which thousands of French soldiers died. He realized the Americas were not crucial to France.[29] The British navy was trouble

---

[28] Mark, H. W. (2023, July 6). Coronation of Napoleon I. Retrieved from World History Encyclopedia.com: https://www.worldhistory.org/article/2251/coronation-of-napoleon-i/.

[29] Britannica, T. E. (2024, May 23). Haitian Revolution. Retrieved from Britannica.com:

enough without having to defend extensive overseas colonies.

The Coalition Wars

The Napoleonic Wars are also called the Coalition Wars because several coalitions were formed to fight off France. Sometimes, an important power would take a time-out and watch as others struggled to find a way to beat Napoleon.

The reasons for each war varied. However, there were common themes in almost all of them. These motivations help us understand the concern Europe had about Napoleon.

- Political and Diplomatic Reasons

  European powers longed for the status quo. The nations did not want one state to dominate the continent. The French Revolution threatened this balance, and it was then substantially challenged when Napoleon scored victory after victory in the wars.

  Napoleon created satellite states that challenged the authority of larger powers, such as Austria. Napoleon went further by putting family members on the thrones of these new states.

  European monarchs believed revolutionary ideas would lead to the creation of republics. Abolishing the monarchy would threaten the power of the ruling classes. There was already a complicated tradition of alliances and royal marriages in place, which meant the European monarchs were somewhat close to each other.

- Economic and Military Concerns

  Napoleon eventually create the Continental System to severely restrict commerce, especially to Great Britain. This system would convince Russia to steer away from allying with France, as the country's economic difficulties gradually outweighed neutrality or forming an alliance with France.

  The military threat posed by the French was quite real. France's mass conscription and novel military tactics triumphed over traditional European ways of fighting wars, and the coalition armies were not prepared to effectively counter Napoleon's military genius.

---

https://www.britannica.com/topic/Haitian-Revolution

France was a social laboratory in the early 19th century. Removing traditional hierarchies, introducing new legal codes, and refining administrative practices made the European social elite consider these innovations as threats to their way of life, encouraging them to join together in alliances.

To summarize, it was a fight between the new and the old. The Ancien Régime was dying, but there were still rulers who wanted to continue a social and political order that benefited them. The reasons for forming coalitions would change over the years, but it appears that the old aristocracy of Europe was terrified of Napoleon and would go to any length to stop him.

A portrait of Napoleon.[viii]

The War of the Third Coalition (1805-1806): The Cause

Napoleon's growing influence in Italy and Germany was alarming, particularly to Austria. There was a general worry that Bonaparte would not stop what he was doing and might influence disgruntled subjects into rebelling. There was an isolated incident that further provoked a response.

Louis Antoine, Duke of Enghien, was a member of the House of Bourbon. He wanted to overturn the results of the French Revolution. There was a conspiracy called the Cadoudal Affair, which was uncovered in August 1803. The plotters planned to either kidnap or assassinate Napoleon. The duke was suspected of being part of the plot, and Napoleon ordered his arrest. Even though the Bourbon prince was living in Baden, he was kidnapped by French soldiers and returned to France, where he was tried and eventually executed. His death prompted Austria and Russia to join in opposing Napoleon.

Great Britain declared war on France on May 18th, 1803. Napoleon retaliated by seizing the Electorate of Hanover and organizing an invasion of England. He assembled an army and tried to coordinate an Irish rebellion to distract the British. He had gathered 120,000 men at Boulogne by early spring 1804.

The rest of Europe had been sitting on the sidelines, but the execution of the duke of Enghien, Napoleon's coronation as emperor, and the annexation of Piedmont and Elba in 1805, which was in direct violation of treaties with Austria, alarmed Europeans to the point where other powers were willing to join Great Britain in a coalition against Napoleon.

British Prime Minister William Pitt started to shop for alliances. By August 1805, the Third Coalition had Great Britain, Sweden, Russia, Austria, Naples, and Sicily as members. Napoleon had its German client states of Baden, Württemberg, Bavaria, the Batavian Republic, the Kingdom of Italy, Etruria, and Spain.

The Third Coalition's plan of attack was for Austria to send an army into Italy. A second army would march on Bavaria. Russia was supposed to reinforce the army attacking Bavaria. Unfortunately, the Russians were impeded by poor roads in eastern Europe and moved slowly. They would not be available for an extended period, which helped the French emperor.

The Grande Armée's Quick Step

Napoleon was not waiting for things to happen. He canceled his plans to invade England to respond to the situation in Europe. He ordered an army to advance into Italy to check the Austrians there. Napoleon began moving rapidly with the rest of the army, crossing the Rhine on September 25th, 1805. This surprised the Third Coalition, who thought that Napoleon would not abandon the invasion of England. They were now dealing with a French army numbering close to 210,000 men in central Germany that was headed rapidly eastward. The Austrian army, under Austrian General Karl Mack von Leiberich, had approximately seventy-two thousand men.

Napoleon's advance through Germany demonstrated how quickly the French army could move. He did not have to worry about supply wagons because his troops were living off the land, and the corps were moving semi-independently from each other. Napoleon covered considerable ground, more than an ordinary army of the time could. Within eleven days, on October 7th, 1805, the French were at the banks of the Danube. Mack would have a difficult time responding to this.[30]

Napoleon was leaving no stone unturned, and he had excellent intelligence. Reconnaissance and a network of spies kept him informed of his enemies' movements, so he had a good understanding of the readiness of the Austrian troops. Armed with this particular, Napoleon was able to make his next move.

The Ulm Campaign

Mack was not as well informed as Napoleon. The Austrian general was still waiting for the Russians to arrive. Mack thought that the French army was not bigger than his. He had no idea that Napoleon was advancing with a force that was nearly three times larger than his own.

Napoleon crossed the Danube unnoticed by Mack. The Grande Armée was screened by its cavalry and moved to the rear of the Austrian force, effectively cutting off any possibility of retreat. Through several engagements, Napoleon gradually forced the Austrians to move to the city of Ulm by October 15th. French artillery started firing the following day, and Mack realized he and his men were surrounded. There was no sign of the Russians. Mack knew the situation was hopeless. So, he

---

[30] Mark, H. W. (2023, July 18). War of the Third Coalition. Retrieved from World History Encyclopedia: https://www.worldhistory.org/War_of_the_Third_Coalition/.

surrendered on October 20th. Napoleon had won the campaign without having to fight a major battle.[31]

An illustration of Mack surrendering to Napoleon.[ix]

The Third Coalition was defeated, but it was not out of the fight. The Russians, under Mikhail Kutuzov, finally reached the agreed-upon rendezvous point, but they retreated. The road to Vienna was open, and Napoleon entered the Austrian capital on November 13th, 1805. The Austrians and Russians regrouped at Olmutz and had ninety thousand men ready to fight. In addition, Austrian Archduke Charles was coming up from Italy with eighty thousand men. Napoleon had to move quickly, or else he would be overwhelmed by a superior force.

Ready to Deceive

The Coalition army planned to cut off Napoleon from his lines of communication and force him into a decisive battle. Napoleon used a strategy of deception to confuse his enemy. He halted his forward movement and allowed the Coalition to react. Kutuzov advanced, and Napoleon led the Russian commander on by moving several miles southeast of Brunn. He was able to disguise the movement of his troops, and he concentrated nearly seventy-three thousand men behind the Goldbach River.

---

[31] Britannica, E. o. (2024, May 14). Battle of Ulm. Retrieved from Britannica.com: https://www.britannica.com/event/Battle-of-Ulm.

Napoleon did everything in his power to deceive the Russians into thinking that the French were in a weak position and vulnerable to attack. He used disinformation to paint a picture of low French morale and added to that by openly talking about possibly retreating out of the area. His schemes worked. The Third Coalition forces began maneuvering into position for a battle. The drama would take place at Austerlitz, a town located in what is now the Czech Republic.

Battle of Austerlitz

The Battle of Austerlitz is commonly known as the Battle of the Three Emperors, as Emperor Francis of Austria, Tsar Alexander of Russia, and Emperor Napoleon Bonaparte were present. The French were outnumbered; Austria and Russia had approximately ninety thousand troops in position. The Coalition commanders were confident of a victory thanks to Napoleon's deceptive activity. They would meet in a council of war on December 1st, 1805, to decide what to do the following day.

Emperor Francis and Kutuzov wanted to take a cautious approach. Alexander, on the other hand, was spoiling for a fight. It was finally decided that an attack would be made on the French right flank. Most of the Coalition troops would be deployed in that area. They did not know that Napoleon had deliberately weakened that point in his line to encourage an assault. The Pratzen Heights were strategically positioned, and Napoleon abandoned that high ground to further entice an enemy attack. The battle began the next day on December 2nd.

The Coalition forces took the bait and launched a major assault on the Pratzen Heights. In doing so, they caused their right flank and center to be vulnerable. The Coalition forces captured the Pratzen Heights, but Napoleon ordered a counterattack with his reserves, which overwhelmed the Coalition army. Napoleon turned his attention to the south and forced the Coalition army back. Gradually, the Coalition soldiers panicked, and they abandoned the field. The fight was over. The French had won.[32]

Austerlitz was the most significant victory Napoleon and his army won in the Napoleonic Wars. Austria signed a truce with France on December 4th, and the Treaty of Pressburg, signed on December 26th,

---

[32] New World Encyclopedia. (2024, June 4). Battle of Austerlitz. Retrieved from New World Encyclopedia.org: https://www.newworldencyclopedia.org/entry/Battle_of_Austerlitz.

ended Austria's involvement. Napoleon had no desire to pursue the Russians, so Alexander and his army were allowed to go home with their tails tucked firmly between their legs. Napoleon had destroyed a larger enemy in only three months.

The War of the Third Coalition showcased Napoleon's Grande Armée and its ability to be a lethal fighting force. If his enemies had not been afraid of him before, they were certainly terrified of him now.

Napoleon Bonaparte had so far proven to be invincible on the battlefield. Fighting on the water was a different story, though.

Chapter 5: The Battle of Trafalgar: Napoleon's Defeat at Sea

Great Britain was proud of its navy, which was the finest in the world. The nation also relied on its ships as the front line of defense. Great Britain shared no borders with other nations, but the vast ocean guaranteed the country could be attacked from anywhere. The fleet had to be ready to respond to any possible threat.

The Royal Navy had to be in state-of-the-art condition to be ready, which meant keeping up with trends and introducing innovations before other navies. The Napoleonic Wars produced technological changes on the sea as well as on land. The Royal Navy responded accordingly.

A significant development occurred in the naval dockyards, especially those in Portsmouth. Great Britain invested heavily in creating wet and dry docks, which allowed the navy to speed up the repair of ships. In addition, British sailors were trained to do repair work at sea so that fighting vessels were constantly on active duty.[33]

The primary artillery piece used by the Royal Navy was the carronade. This was a smoothbore cast iron cannon that was first introduced in the 1770s. It was a short-range, anti-ship, anti-crew weapon. Its range was about half that of a long gun, and it used a much smaller propellant charge to fire cannonballs and shot. This wasn't a

---

[33] Hicks, P. (2024, June 4). The Royal Navy, 1793-1802. Retrieved from Napoleon.org: https://www.napoleon.org/en/history-of-the-two-empires/articles/the-british-navy-1793-1802/.

problem because short-range broadsides were standard naval tactics. Because this artillery piece was lighter and required a small gun crew, it permitted a ship of the line to carry more guns.[34]

There was a pressing need to construct larger ships that would be able to carry more cannons. A standard warship would have two full gun decks, with the upper deck carrying 24-pounders and the lower deck having 32-pounders. Three gun decks were not uncommon.

The HMS *Victory* is an example of a first-rate ship.[35] It had 104 guns. Other ships, such as the HMS *Royal Sovereign* and the HMS *Britannia*, had one hundred guns. The effect of a broadside from any of these warships was devastating.[36] The Royal Navy did have other kinds of warships and sloops with 12- or 24-pounder guns; these were often used to track down privateers on the open water.

The Royal Navy was using better chronometers during the Napoleonic Wars than other nations, which increased the effectiveness of the fleet. Its battle tactics were also aggressive. An excellent example is the Royal Navy's conduct at Trafalgar, which we will cover in just a moment.

Press-ganging, the kidnapping of men to serve on ships, was a common practice, but there were some advantages for a person to volunteer. The Royal Navy protected a man from creditors if the debt was less than £20. This meant that by joining the navy, a man with debt could avoid landing in a debtor's prison. Parliament passed the Quota Acts to guarantee that the navy had sufficient manpower. Every county had to supply a quota of men to the navy. It was also common practice that a convicted criminal could be given the option of going to jail or serving in the navy. Great Britain did whatever was necessary to get men on board ships.[37]

These men had to be led by good officers and commanders who knew what they were doing. Great Britain conducted several major naval operations during the Napoleonic Wars. Its greatest resource was a man

---

[34] A ship of the line was an enormous floating artillery battery. They were the dominant warships of their time.

[35] A first-rate ship is the largest ship in the Royal Navy fleet.

[36] Ernest McNeil Eller, R. L. (2024, June 4). Ships of the Line. Retrieved from Britannica.com: https://www.britannica.com/technology/naval-ship/Ship-of-the-line.

[37] Hicks, P. The Royal Navy, 1793-1802.

who stood out for his nautical brilliance.

Horatio the Great

The Napoleonic Wars produced two men of unique military genius. They never met each other in battle, but both contributed significantly to the art of warfare. The first was Napoleon Bonaparte. The second was a sailor named Horatio Nelson.

The poet Lord Byron called him "Britannia's God of War." Horatio Nelson is considered the greatest naval commander in British history. His seamanship was the stuff of legend, which makes sense. After all, Nelson almost single-handedly frustrated Napoleon's efforts to invade Great Britain.

Nelson was born on September 18th, 1758, in Norfolk and used family connections to join the navy when he was only twelve years old. Sea voyages took young Nelson to the West Indies and the North Sea while he was still a teenager. In a time when talent meant more than years, Nelson was given command of the HMS *Badger*. He was only twenty years old.

In the last years of the 18th century, the Royal Navy was enormous. Over 660 ships flew the Union Jack, which was more than the navies of France and Spain combined. Roughly 100,000 men were in the ranks. That impressive number represented a challenge for ambitious men like Horatio Nelson.[38] All of these ships meant there were thousands of officers trying to advance in their naval careers. It would not be easy for Nelson because he did not have the years of service or aristocratic connections that others enjoyed. He would have to find another way to the top.

Of course, one way to do that is to get into the thick of a battle and risk getting killed. Horatio Nelson was not afraid. Indeed, he was known for his incredible courage and was the kind of officer who led from the front. His personal courage came at a price, though. Nelson lost an eye and an arm, among other injuries, while defending his country.

He became known as someone who inspired loyalty in the officers he commanded. Nelson was particularly close to the captains of the ships in his fleet. He referred to them as his band of brothers, and they looked up to him with love and respect. Nelson's ability to connect with his men

---

[38] Hicks, P. The Royal Navy, 1793-1802.

and be brave in the face of enemy fire allowed him to advance to the highest ranks in the Royal Navy.[39]

A portrait of Horatio Nelson.*

Excellent Mentors

Two exceptional men shaped Horatio Nelson's outlook on war and battle tactics. The first was his uncle, who helped get Nelson into the navy in the first place. Captain Maurice Suckling coached his nephew on

---

[39] Setterfield, R. (2019, November 18). Horatio Nelson: From Frail Boy to National Hero. Retrieved from Onthisday.com: https://www.onthisday.com/articles/horatio-nelson-from-frail-boy-to-national-hero.

the significance of understanding gun tactics and how crucial good seamanship was for success. Nelson's early years at sea included time in the Mediterranean and service during the American Revolutionary War. He served under Admiral Lord Hood. Thanks to Hood, Nelson received command experience and was exposed to various naval strategies and battle tactics. Surprise and aggression were two primary lessons he learned. By the time the French Revolution had broken out, Horatio Nelson had been in the navy for nearly twenty years. Almost half of that time had been spent as the commander of a ship. He was a well-seasoned veteran.

Fighting the Revolutionary French

At the start of the French Revolution, the Royal Navy vessels were the wooden walls protecting Great Britain from any major invasion. The navy also was responsible for protecting trade routes, which were essential for Great Britain's economic survival.

There were encounters with the French during this time. The first was the Battle of Ushant, also known as the Glorious First of June, fought on June 1st, 1794, at the southwestern end of the English Channel. A grain convoy was sailing toward France, and the British fleet under Lord Richard Howe moved to intercept it. Both sides claimed victory; the British sunk seven French ships, but the French were able to get the grain convoy through friendly ports.

A tactical innovation made this battle memorable. Ordinarily, opposing fleets would line up in a row facing each other and proceed to blast away. The British commander Lord Howe did something different. Instead of forming a battle line, Howe ordered his ships to attack the French directly. Every British ship was ordered to engage the enemy ship closest to it, which surprised the French.

Another significant battle was the Battle of Cape St. Vincent, which took place on February 14th, 1797. This was an encounter between the British fleet, commanded by Admiral John Jervis, and the Spanish fleet off Cape St. Vincent, Portugal. Nelson was a principal player in this engagement.

Displaying his trademark audacity, Nelson acted independently and broke out from the British line to attack Spanish ships. He sailed into the enemy squadrons and, at one time, at least according to legend, was fighting seven Spanish vessels. Nelson personally boarded and captured one ship and then boarded and took another. His actions earned him a knighthood, and he became a national celebrity. He was also promoted to rear admiral.[40]

Battle of the Nile

This engagement, also known as the Battle of Aboukir Bay, was fought from August 1st to August 3rd, 1798. Nelson chased a French fleet carrying an expeditionary force under Napoleon Bonaparte to invade Egypt. He was hot on the tail of the French ships and missed catching up to them several times. The French were able to land in Egypt and anchored in Aboukir Bay.

As soon as Nelson spotted the French vessels, he ordered an attack. He split his fleet into two squadrons, one passing between the French and the shore and the other striking from the seaward side. The French fleet was destroyed, and Napoleon was stranded in Egypt. Nelson had again shown his audacity.

Battle of Copenhagen

The Battle of Copenhagen was fought on April 2nd, 1801, in the harbor of the Danish capital.

The League of Armed Neutrality was an alliance whose members were Denmark, Sweden, Prussia, and Russia. Its intention was to protect the member nations' trade and cut Great Britain off from valuable timber supplies. A British fleet was sent to the Baltic to break the coalition and neutralize the Danish Navy.

There was an attempt to diplomatically resolve the problems, but it went nowhere. Nelson decided to act and launch an attack on Danish and Norwegian ships protected by shore batteries. He was ordered by the British commanding admiral, Sir Hyde Parker, to disengage. A legend of the battle says that Parker placed the signal to Nelson, ordering Nelson to break off the attack. Nelson was blind in one eye and was looking through his telescope using his blind eye. He claimed he didn't see Parker's signal and continued the fight. Eventually, the British admiral was successful and negotiated an indefinite armistice. Once again, Horatio Nelson was the man of the hour.

---

[40] Pock, T. (2024, June 4). Battles of Cape St. Vincent and the Nile. Retrieved from Britannica.com: https://www.britannica.com/biography/Horatio-Nelson/Battles-of-Cape-St-Vincent-and-the-Nile.

A Grand Deception

Trafalgar is recognized as one of the fifteen most decisive battles in world history. It was an epic confrontation between the Royal Navy and the combined Franco-Spanish fleet. It had an impact on the Napoleonic Wars, and it was the capstone of Horatio Nelson's career. This battle was not an isolated event but rather part of a strategy that, if it succeeded, might have resulted in Napoleon's invasion and conquest of Great Britain.

A sort of arms race occurred in the early 19th century. The British had naval superiority, and the French were trying to match the size of the Royal Navy. The French were able to come close to that by bullying Spain into an alliance that allowed the French and Spanish fleets to be combined. The possibility of matching the British one on one would help Napoleon in one of his most ambitious military plans.

Napoleon wanted Great Britain out of the way. He considered the British to be a nuisance and a distraction to his Continental plans. Unfortunately for him, the ocean protected the island country. Bonaparte would need to neutralize the British fleet long enough to launch a massive invasion of Great Britain. He had an idea that he was convinced might work.

Napoleon planned to trick the Royal Navy into making Britain vulnerable to attack. What the French emperor had in mind was for the French fleet based in Toulon to run the British blockade of that port and get out into the open waters of the Mediterranean. From there, the French would rendezvous with the Spanish fleet and sail toward the Caribbean. Napoleon gambled that the British would take the bait and chase the Franco-Spanish fleet to the Americas. Eventually, the Franco-Spanish ships would turn and speed back to the English Channel and meet up with French and Spanish squadrons. Napoleon would thus have control of the English Channel for a few days until the pursuing British ships arrived. Those few days would be enough for Napoleon to transport his massive army in Boulogne across the Channel and invade England.

The commander of the French fleet, Vice Admiral Pierre-Charles de Villeneuve, sailed out of Toulon in late March 1805. Nelson, who was commanding ships in the Mediterranean, thought the French were headed toward Egypt. He later found out they were headed toward the West Indies and pursued them, but the French had a three-week head start.

Villeneuve made it to Martinique but then turned around to head back to Europe when he discovered that Nelson had arrived in the Caribbean. Instead of heading straight for the English Channel, the French admiral sailed his ships to Cádiz, Spain.[41]

Villeneuve's ships anchored in the Cádiz harbor, and Nelson established a blockade. Napoleon became angry with Villeneuve and ordered the admiral to break out of Cádiz, sail to Naples, and support French activity in Italy. Villeneuve hesitated and spent the late summer trapped in the Spanish port. He finally received word that he was in danger of being replaced, which prompted him to take action. He ordered his fleet to sail on October 19th, 1805.

Nelson was aware of what Villeneuve was doing and prepared his ships. He ordered a general chase, and on October 21st, the British fleet was only a few miles away from the Franco-Spanish ships. Villeneuve had thirty-three ships of the line, and Nelson had twenty-seven. Despite being outnumbered, Nelson had supreme confidence in the men and officers he commanded. At 11:48 a.m., he hoisted the signals that were later memorialized: "England expects that every man will do his duty."

There was a following message: "Engage the enemy more closely."[42]

The engagement was about to begin.

The Battle of Trafalgar

Horatio Nelson rarely played by the book, and his battle plan was not standard. He would not set his ships in a line parallel to the enemy for broadsides. Instead, Nelson split his ships into two columns and instructed his captains to break through the opposing line perpendicularly. This would make close-quarters combat easier to perform, and that was where the British sailors were best. It would be a tricky maneuver, but Nelson had great faith in his captains.

Nelson led one column in his flagship, HMS *Victory*, and broke through the enemy line. The battle quickly turned into single-ship engagements, and the HMS *Victory* attacked the French flagship, the

---

[41] Encyclopedia.com. (2018, May 23). Battle of Trafalgar. Retrieved from Encyclopedia.com: https://www.encyclopedia.com/history/modern-europe/wars-and-battles/battle-trafalgar.

[42] Royal Navy. (2024, June 4). Trafalgar Day. Retrieved from Royalnavy.mod.uk: https://www.royalnavy.mod.uk/news-and-latest-activity/events/national/171021-trafalgar-day.

Bucentaure. Nelson's attack on the enemy's flagship disrupted the communications of the Franco-Spanish fleet. The battle raged all afternoon on October 21st. Villeneuve surrendered at 1:45 p.m., and the struggle ended by 4:30 p.m. Nelson had won a stunning victory. It would be his last.

The vice admiral was walking the deck of his ship when he was cut down by a French sniper firing from the *Redoubtable* at approximately 1:15 p.m. The bullet went through Nelson's shoulder and chest. He received word that the British won the battle, and his last words were, "Now I am satisfied. Thank God I have done my duty." With that, the greatest naval commander in British history died.[43]

Horatio Nelson had given his eye, an arm, and his life in the service of his country. The Franco-Spanish fleet at Trafalgar suffered a terrible defeat. Twenty-two ships were captured or destroyed. The British did not lose one ship.

The consequences of the victory were significant. Great Britain had total control of the sea, and Napoleon's plan to invade Great Britain was destroyed. The French navy would not be a significant factor in the rest of the Napoleonic Wars. Napoleon would turn his attention to mainland Europe. Although the French lost at Trafalgar, they were winning on land. For instance, Napoleon would win at Austerlitz just a few weeks later. His star was still ascending, but he would eventually make a major mistake.

---

[43] Pocock, T. (2024, June 4). Horatio Nelson at Trafalgar. Retrieved from Britannica.com: https://www.britannica.com/biography/Horatio-Nelson/Victory-at-Trafalgar.

Chapter 6: Napoleon's Zenith

The ink was barely dry on the treaty that ended the War of the Third Coalition before another alliance was created to oppose France. The Fourth Coalition included Prussia, Russia, Great Britain, Saxony, and Sweden. Each had their reasons for seeking a fight with Napoleon. The agenda of each reflects the political dynamics that were taking place in Europe and the threat that Napoleon posed to the status quo.

Prussia Steps In

Prussia stayed out of the wars of the Second and Third Coalitions, watching events develop from the safety of neutrality. Not taking sides was a good idea, but it did not sit well with the Prussian upper class and military. These aristocrats and generals believed that Prussia had to play a dominant role in German affairs, and Napoleon's creation of the Confederation of the Rhine disturbed them. They were champing at the bit to reassert Prussian influence in central Europe.

The Curse of Frederick

Frederick the Great was a military genius. He reigned in the 18th century. His battle tactics and strategies in the War of the Austrian Succession and later in the Seven Years' War were admired and studied. Prussia's reputation for martial excellence stemmed from Frederick's achievements. In 1806, this proved to be an albatross around Prussia's neck.

Twenty years after Frederick's death, the Prussian military had changed very little. The generals adhered to the battle tactics of the great king and did not see any reason to change. Frederick's deeds made the

Prussians overconfident. They were convinced that a well-disciplined Prussian army was more than a match for a crowd of French conscripts.

The Prussians were making a terrible mistake, though. Prussian soldiers had not been in combat since 1795, while the French regiments had almost constantly fought. If nothing else, the French were seasoned veterans. The Prussians, however, still believed they would be superior on the battlefield, and they also believed in their own legends.

There was also the matter of national honor. Many Prussians, especially those in the officer corps, felt humiliated by not participating in the earlier coalition wars. These people believed they could have made a difference and stopped Napoleon. The Prussians had not paid close attention to the French and were confidently walking into a disaster.

Russia

Russia was still at war with France when the Fourth Coalition was formed. The Russians had been beaten at Austerlitz, so they knew of the strength of the French army. Nevertheless, Russia was concerned about the creation of the Confederation of the Rhine and France's growing influence in Europe. The tsar's government was worried that Napoleon would extend his interests into eastern Europe, an area that was part of Russia's sphere of influence.[44]

There was also a degree of personal prestige. Tsar Alexander I believed Russia should be a principal player in maintaining the status quo of Europe. He felt that Russia needed to counterbalance Napoleon. Moreover, Alexander had aspirations of military glory despite the Russians' humiliating defeat at Austerlitz.

Great Britain's Sterling Assistance

Great Britain had an enormous navy, but its army was considerably smaller. The Royal Navy could control the sea and protect the trade routes of the Fourth Coalition during the war, but there was something else that Great Britain provided, which was a considerable contribution to the war effort: the pound sterling.

The ravages of war did not touch the British economy, and the country's overseas trade thrived. The French navy could no longer stop

---

[44] Mark, H. W. (2023, July 28). War of the Fourth Coalition. Retrieved from World History Encyclopedia: https://www.worldhistory.org/War_of_the_Fourth_Coalition/.

British ships from carrying goods overseas, and Great Britain had the financial means to conduct a war without suffering significant casualties.

The British banking system was superior to anything on the Continent. It was able to subsidize its allies without straining the economy. Government loans and taxes were used to finance the costs incurred in the Napoleonic Wars, which, by the end of the conflicts, totaled over £1.6 billion. Great Britain could not provide large armies until later in the war, but its financial support was worth an entire army corps.[45]

The British involvement in the Fourth Coalition continued its hostility with France. That mutual animosity was sufficient for Great Britain to ally against France, and checking Napoleon's expansionism was part of British national policy.

The Others

Sweden played a minor role in the Fourth Coalition. Its primary concern was to counterbalance Napoleon and preserve Sweden's dominant role in northern Europe. Saxony was in the war as an ally of Prussia and would later change sides.

The War Begins

Prussia issued an ultimatum to Napoleon on October 1st, 1806. The Prussians demanded that all French troops on the west side of the Rhine be removed. Furthermore, Napoleon was to recognize the North German Confederation, which Prussia dominated. Napoleon was willing to acknowledge the confederation, but the war party in Prussia was demanding action. On October 9th, 1806, King Frederick William III of Prussia formally declared war on France.

The terms of Prussia's ultimatum suggest that it was worded to leave Napoleon little choice but to ignore it, thereby giving a legitimate reason for Prussia to declare war. In any event, the declaration was strategically a mistake. There were already French troops in Germany. Napoleon could immediately respond. In fact, Napoleon had anticipated the declaration of war, and on October 8th, the Grande Armée crossed over into Saxony. The actual fighting started earlier than the Prussians were

---

[45] Colley, L. J. (2024, June 8). The Napoleonic Wars. Retrieved from Britannica.com: https://www.britannica.com/place/United-Kingdom/The-Napoleonic-Wars.

expecting.[46]

Prussia underestimated how quickly the Grande Armée could move. Conventional warfare assumed it would take several weeks before major armies could face each other. Prussia would be taking on France without Russia's support, which was still re-mobilizing.

Napoleon marched his army in three separate columns to southern Thuringia. Each corps was within easy support distance of the other, permitting the French military to be flexible enough to meet the enemy under any conditions. The first contact between the Prussians and the French was on October 9th, 1806, at the Battle of Schleiz, and there was another engagement on October 10th at Saalfeld.[47]

The Prussians followed their traditional military procedures and were caught off guard by Napoleon's quick movement. The Prussians lost their popular commander, Prince Louis Ferdinand, at the Battle of Saalfeld and retreated to Jena.

Battle of Jena-Auerstedt

The war was only five days old when the decisive Battle of Jena-Auerstedt occurred on October 14th.

To take advantage of the field at Jena-Auerstedt, Napoleon had his corps execute a flanking movement north and east. One corps under Marshal Louis-Nicolas Davout outmaneuvered the Prussians and defeated them. Prussian attempts to successfully counterattack failed, and Frederick William III eventually ordered a withdrawal. Marshal Murat's cavalry pursued the retreating Prussians. Thousands of Prussians were either captured or cut down.

The Prussians suffered a total defeat in these two battles. The French pursued the beaten army, preventing it from regrouping to counterattack. Napoleon entered Berlin, Prussia's capital, on October 24th, 1806. Frederick William III still wanted to fight and fled to Königsberg. What was left of the Prussian army was gradually destroyed, as the French marshals, Bernadotte, Soult, and Marat, pursued them. Prussian General Gebhard von Blücher surrendered his command on November 7th,

---

[46] Mark, H. W. War of the Fourth Coalition.

[47] Anonymous. (2024, June 8). War of the Fourth Coalition. Retrieved from Resources.saylor.org: https://resources.saylor.org/wwwresources/archived/site/wp-content/uploads/2011/05/War-of-the-Fourth-coalition.pdf.

1806, as Lübeck fell to the French.[48]

The Berlin Decree, issued on November 21ˢᵗ, 1806, highlighted Napoleon's stay in Berlin. This imperial order ordered an embargo on all British trade goods in those territories controlled or allied to the French. The French emperor also used this time to come to an understanding with the Electorate of Saxony. Saxony joined the Confederation of the Rhine and was subsequently made a German kingdom.[49]

The Polish Campaign

The Prussians were eliminated as an effective threat, but the Russians remained. The Russians could not assist the Prussians earlier, but by December 1806, Russian troops had been sent to reinforce what was left of the Prussian resistance. The Russian force numbered nearly eighty thousand men. There were still some logistical problems, and the rapid French advance caused the troops to move before they were ready, but the Russians were on the march. They were under the command of General Levin August von Bennigsen. The fighting to come would take place in Poland and East Prussia.[50]

Poland had endured the humiliation of being gradually partitioned out of existence in 1772, 1793, and 1795. Napoleon entered Warsaw on December 19ᵗʰ to the sound of cheering crowds. The Polish hoped the French emperor would restore the Polish nation.

This was a unique opportunity for Napoleon. He could punish the Prussians by taking the land seized in the partitions and create a client state that bordered Russia. Accordingly, Napoleon established the Grand Duchy of Warsaw, which would be governed by a new French ally, Frederick Augustus, King of Saxony.

Operations against the Russians

Even today, winter is a terrible time of the year to campaign. Napoleon ordered his troops forward to cross the Vistula River and gain ground before winter set in. The French moved forward under poor

---

[48] Mark, H. W. (2023, June 19). Battle of Jena-Auerstedt. Retrieved from World History Encyclopedia: https://www.worldhistory.org/article/2256/battle-of-jena-auerstedt/.

[49] Mark, H. W. Battle of Jena-Auerstedt.

[50] Napoleon & Empire. (2024, May 14). Battle of Eylau. Retrieved from Napoleon &Empire.net: https://www.napoleon-empire.net/en/battles/eylau.php.

traveling conditions and fought a Russian force at Pultusk on December 26th. Both sides went into winter quarters after that; they would not meet again until February 1807.[51]

Battle of Eylau

Napoleon fought two battles with the Russians in the Fourth War of the Coalition. The first Franco-Russian confrontation took place in the town of Eylau on February 7th, 1807. The French army comprised approximately fifty thousand men, and the Russians had sixty-five thousand.

Napoleon wanted a decisive confrontation with the Russians and planned to strike quickly with an insurmountable force. The Russians might have learned something from the defeat at Austerlitz, though. Despite outnumbering the French, the Russian commander, Bennigsen, took a defensive position. He hoped that the French assault on his lines would expose weaknesses that the Russians could then exploit.

The main battle began on February 8th. The two sides started with an artillery duel that lasted for several hours. Both sides attacked and counterattacked, with the French and Russians giving ground only after a fierce resistance. At one point, there was hand-to-hand fighting in the town's streets. The Russians came close to seizing Napoleon's headquarters; the French emperor was even at risk of being captured. All of this happened during a winter blizzard.

The decisive moment in the battle came with an enormous cavalry charge led by Murat. The chaos that ensued among the Russians permitted Napoleon to re-form his lines. The timely arrival of Russian reinforcements prevented a rout. The battle eventually ended late at night on February 8th. It ended as a draw, with both sides suffering heavy casualties.[52]

The Russians proved they could stand up to the French. Napoleon expected to overwhelm them, but the Russians' use of defensive positions and timely counterattacks prevented that from happening. Moreover, the Russians retreated in good order and would fight the French again.

---

[51] Mark, H. W. (2023, July 24). Battle of Eylau. Retrieved from World History Encyclopedia: https://www.worldhistory.org/article/2258/battle-of-eylau/.

[52] Mark, H. W. Battle of Eylau.

Battle of Friedland

Eylau was not the smashing victory that Napoleon had hoped to obtain. The Grande Armée needed some time to rest and resupply. Napoleon decided to wait until the regular fighting season began once again. In the meantime, he asked for reinforcements from French allies and called for French conscripts to arrive early. Skirmishes were fought between the French and the Russians in the following weeks. Danzig fell to the French on May 24th, 1807. Reinforcements flowed in, and Napoleon was ready to return on the offensive. He decided that June 10th would be the day to start moving forward. The Russians forced him to change his mind.

Bennigsen saw an opportunity. He attacked Field Marshal Ney's corps at Guttstadt-Deppen. The Russians were beaten, and Napoleon decided to cut Bennigsen from his supply base in Königsberg. He used a deceptive tactic; he permitted a messenger to be captured by the Russians. The French soldier was carrying false news that the Grande Armée was about to launch an attack on the Russian rearguard. Bennigsen took the bait and moved his troops to a well-defended position at Heilsberg. On June 10th, Napoleon attacked, but the Russians won a tactical victory. Bennigsen went on the offensive and crossed the Alle River to fight the French on the western bank. He did not realize that he was walking into a trap.

Marshal Lannes led his corps to confront the Russians on the morning of June 14th, 1807, pulling the Russians back long enough to allow Napoleon to bring the rest of the army into position. He ordered an artillery barrage that covered an attack by Marshal Ney's corps on the Russian left flank. Bennigsen ordered a cavalry counterattack, but Ney was reinforced before his line broke. French artillery raked the Russian lines, and the French infantry pressed the Russians up against the banks of the river. Ultimately, Bennigsen ordered a general retreat, and what was left of the Russian army marched (or swam) back over the Alle. Napoleon had won a significant victory.[53]

The Russians fought with considerable courage against superior forces in all of the battles. Their major problem in each engagement was their inability to respond to quick changes on the battlefield. Napoleon's

---

[53] Mark, H. W. (2023, July 25). Battle of Friedland. Retrieved from World History Encyclopedia: https://www.worldhistory.org/article/2259/battle-of-friedland/.

army could move rapidly. One corps could come to the aid of the other before the Russians could effectively respond. There was no doubting the bravery of the Russian soldiers, but changes needed to be made if they could have any hope of defeating Napoleon.

The fighting was over. The allies of the Fourth Coalition could not field an army to meet the French adequately, and a peace treaty had to be hammered out. It was expected that the terms would be to Napoleon's advantage.

Napoleon intended to complete France's domination of Europe at the expense of any remaining rivals. He wanted his new Continental System to be recognized by all of Europe, and he hoped that would be sufficient enough to bring Great Britain to its knees. The Holy Roman Empire, which had lasted for nearly a thousand years as a dominant presence in central Europe, would be relegated to the dustbin of history. Napoleon wanted a European map consisting of either allies or satellite states.

However, a primary concern was Russia. Despite the losses, Russia was still a significant power and could field large armies. Napoleon wanted to neutralize any possible future threat Russia might pose, making any further coalitions against France impossible.

Napoleon and Alexander

The Russian town of Tilsit would be the scene of the negotiations. Napoleon and Alexander conferred on a raft in the middle of the Nieman River on June 25th, 1807. The meeting between the two emperors was one of mutual respect and an understanding of the needs both had. In retrospect, Napoleon was more than generous.

In return for joining the Continental System, France would aid Russia in its disputes against the Ottoman Empire. Alexander agreed to evacuate Wallachia and Moldavia and give France the Ionian islands and the town of Cattaro (now Kotor, Montenegro). Napoleon compensated for the losses by recognizing the sovereignty of the Duchy of Oldenburg in addition to other small countries in Germany that belonged to Alexander's relatives. The peace treaty between France and Russia was formalized on July 7th, 1807.

A French medallion showing the two rulers embracing each other.[ii]

To the Victor, the Spoils. To the Loser, the Costs

Prussia did not get off easy. Napoleon was in no mood to be kind to the enemy who started the fight. Frederick William III would lose nearly half of his nation. The client states that Napoleon wanted to create included the Kingdom of Westphalia, the Grand Duchy of Warsaw, and the Free City of Danzig. Bialystok became a Russian possession, and Cottbus now belonged to Saxony. Prussia's army was reduced to only forty-three thousand men, and a monetary tribute was later imposed on Prussia. Frederick William III had no bargaining chips and could only agree to the terms. The Franco-Prussian treaty was formalized on July 9th, 1807.

Prussia paid dearly, both politically and economically, for losing the war. Napoleon probably wanted to demonstrate to the rest of the world that while he could be lenient with a former enemy like Russia, he could be ruthless with another.

Napoleon was at the zenith of his power. He had defeated one European rival and destroyed the other. No sane monarch in Europe would try to go up against him. Great Britain remained a French rival, and hostilities continued between the two nations. The Continent, however, belonged to Napoleon.

Chapter 7: The Peninsular War: Napoleon's Struggle in Spain and Portugal

Napoleon was undoubtedly a genius, but he was also a man. He was human, which means he was capable of making mistakes. Bonaparte was at the height of his power when he started making mistakes that would ultimately bring him down. Three major missteps happened between the years of 1806 and 1808.

The Continental System

Napoleon held the British in contempt, but the Battle of Trafalgar ended his plans of invading Great Britain. So, the French emperor decided to take a different tack. He would destroy British trade and bring his enemy to their knees economically.

He issued the Berlin Decree on November 21st, 1806. This was Napoleon's response to the British blockade that seriously restricted commerce in France and other areas of Europe that France controlled. The decree banned British ships from coming into European ports. Napoleon went a step further on December 17th, 1807, with the Milan Decree. This permitted French warships to seize ships that were sailing from British ports or countries that were under British influence. The Milan Decree forbade European countries from trading with Great

Britain.[54]

Special agencies were established to enforce the decrees and confiscate any British merchandise that were found in the holds of the ships. It was a 19th-century version of the trade sanctions that are commonly used today.

There was another reason for these restrictions. Napoleon wanted to promote French commerce and develop stronger economic relations with the satellite states of Europe. He wanted to develop self-sufficiency in European economies so they did not rely on British manufacturers. Napoleon used his power to force French-controlled nations and allies to comply. In addition, neutral states, such as Denmark, were forced to be part of the Continental System. Russia was required to be a participant because of the Treaty of Tilsit.

Napoleon was seriously mistaken if he thought that he could do permanent damage to Great Britain with the Continental System. British maritime commerce had been well established for centuries. Although there was some initial inconvenience, and adjustments had to be made, Great Britain still engaged in international trade. British merchants made up for any losses caused by the Continental System by increasing trade relations with the Americas and other parts of the world. Moreover, the British produced high-quality goods, which were still in high demand in Europe.

Widespread Noncompliance

It was easy enough to issue decrees, but the hard part was trying to enforce them. The French no longer had a viable navy, and the British were able to protect any ships flying the Union Jack. Smuggling became a major industry under the Continental System. It is estimated that over eight hundred smuggling vessels were operating in the Mediterranean in 1811. Ports such as Thessaloniki and Malta became principal smuggling hubs. Despite the embargo, Great Britain was able to export £10 million worth of goods to southern Europe in 1809.[55]

---

[54] History Skills. (2024, June 10). What Was Napoleon's Revolutionary Continental System and How Did It Shape Modern Europe. Retrieved from Historyskills.com: https://www.historyskills.com/classroom/modern-history/continental-system/.

[55] Mark, H. W. (2023, August 3). Continental System. Retrieved from World History Encyclopedia.com: https://www.worldhistory.org/Continental_System/.

The Continental System had a negative effect on Europe, though. European manufacturers had to deal with the shortage of raw materials, and several major Italian industries came close to bankruptcy. The situation became so bad that the king of Holland refused to enforce the Continental System because of its adverse impact on the Dutch economy. Incidentally, that monarch was Louis Bonaparte, Napoleon's brother. The French Emperor forced Louis to abdicate and annexed Holland to France. However, Louis Bonaparte was not the only European ruler who ignored the restrictions. Joachim Murat, who had once been a French field marshal and became the king of Naples, did nothing to stop the smuggling in his own kingdom.[56]

Furthermore, the Continental System damaged relations with other countries. Portugal refused to be part of it, and Russia eventually withdrew. Even France suffered because of the embargo. Ultimately, Napoleon was forced to issue the St. Cloud Decree that allowed southwestern France and Spain to have a degree of trade with Great Britain and reopen French trade with the United States. Unfortunately, significant damage had already been done. The Continental System would lead to other bad decisions by Napoleon that resulted in costly military campaigns.

Family Ties

Napoleon wanted to have people on the thrones of conquered countries whom he could trust; he did not want to be backstabbed by anyone. The only people Napoleon could trust completely were his family.

Also, even though he had an imperial title, Napoleon wanted to spread the ideas of the French Revolution to other parts of Europe. It would be easier for him to implement these ideals if people he could trust were in power. Napoleon likely believed his family members would also introduce a degree of stability that had been absent in the preceding years.

Whenever his motivations were, Napoleon consistently placed his relatives in charge of European countries. His plan was not entirely successful.

---

[56] Mark, H. W. Continental System.

Here is a short list of who Napoleon entrusted with nations:
- Joseph Bonaparte was originally made the king of Naples and was later made king of Spain.
- Louis Bonaparte was made king of Holland.
- Jerome Bonaparte was made king of Westphalia.
- Elisa and Pauline Bonaparte were not major queens, but Elisa was made princess of Lucca and Piombino (a client state in Italy) and later became grand duchess of Tuscany. Pauline became duchess of Guastalla (a town in Italy).
- Napoleon's youngest sister, Caroline Bonaparte, became queen consort of Naples and Sicily when her husband, Joachim Murat, was made the king.[57]

The record of the Bonaparte family as rulers was mixed. There were times when they were competent, and there were times the Bonapartes fell short of the mark. Joseph showed some ability when he was king of Naples, but his time as king of Spain bordered on disaster. He was not able to perform adequately due to the resistance from the Spanish people. Louis was sympathetic to the Dutch people, and he promoted various projects and reforms to enhance their well-being. However, he got into trouble with Napoleon when he resisted the Continental System. As mentioned, Napoleon finally annexed Holland and forced his brother to abdicate. Although Jerome implemented the Napoleonic Code and got rid of the old privileges of the aristocracy, he was in over his head when it came to financial matters. He was criticized for maintaining an opulent lifestyle and had a terrible time trying to balance the budget. Napoleon's sisters ruled over relatively small territories. Elisa had good administrative skills, but she relied too much on French support.

The Continental System and the need to supply troops for their brother's military campaigns created an economic strain on the countries governed by the Bonapartes. While each tried to be accepted by their subjects, it became increasingly difficult as the demands of the Napoleonic Wars became greater.

---

[57] Napoleon.org. (2020, December). Napoleon I and His Family. Retrieved from Napoleon.org: https://www.napoleon.org/en/young-historians/napodoc/napoleon-i-and-his-family/.

Nationalism was a major stumbling block for the Bonapartes. They were foreigners and had no viable connection to the countries they ruled. It was the French army that kept these people in charge, and if the army moved on, they found they would not be in power for long. Napoleon's inability to appreciate nationalism's ability to inspire fierce emotions would cause him to make a very expensive error in judgment.

The Peninsular War

To talk about the Peninsular War, we have to back up in time a bit. In the late 18th and 19th century, Spain was not the imperial power it had been in the 16th and 17th centuries. The War of the Spanish Succession stripped the country of significant European possessions, and Spain gradually became a backwater in European politics.

It still had its empire, though. The Bourbon rulers took steps to develop Spanish possessions in the Americas and make improvements in colonial administration. Efforts were made to revitalize the mining industry, particularly the extraction of silver. The Free Trade Act of 1778 made it easier for Spanish ports in the Americas to do business with other ports. Improvements were made in the education system, and the demands made for tribute on indigenous people were reduced.

Charles III hoped to use the ideas of the Enlightenment to modernize Spain, but his successor, Charles IV, relied too much on his first secretary of state, Manuel de Godoy, whose policies were unpopular.

The Spanish monarchy was concerned about what was going on in France during the French Revolution. They worried that similar problems could surface in Spain. The execution of Louis XVI convinced Spain to join the First Coalition and wage the War of the Pyrenees (1793-1795) against France. That war concluded with the Treaty of Basel. Spain gave its eastern portion of Hispaniola to

A portrait of Manuel de Godoy.^{xii}

France. A shift in foreign policy resulted as a consequence of the loss. Spain decided to ally itself with the French Republic. The Treaty of San Ildefonso of 1796 made the two countries allies, and Spain agreed to cooperate with France in a war against Great Britain.[58]

The alliance proved to be a mistake for Spain. The nation was involved in the Anglo-Spanish War from 1796 to 1802, and a British blockade deprived Spain of products from the American colonies. Moreover, the Spanish Navy suffered a terrible defeat at the Battle of Cape St. Vincent. The Treaty of Amiens in 1802 provided a truce, but fighting broke out again in 1804. Once again, the Spanish Navy endured devastating losses; this time, it was at Trafalgar. The second round of warfare ended in 1808, but by that time, even more dramatic events were happening on the Iberian Peninsula.

Napoleon was determined to have the Continental System enforced throughout Europe, and that included Portugal and Spain. Portugal refused to join the Continental System because its economy relied on maritime trade. Napoleon was not accustomed to being turned down, and he issued an ultimatum to Portugal, which the Portuguese rejected. Napoleon responded by invading Portugal on November 19th, 1807. This effectively began the Peninsular War.

Spain did its best as an ally to France and suffered for it. Charles IV was a weak king and relied heavily on his prime minister, Manuel de Godoy. The prime minister's policies were not well received by the Spanish people. Many wanted the son of Charles, Ferdinand, to become the king. This led to internal squabbling, which permitted an opportunity for Napoleon.

<u>An Amazing Act of Treachery</u>

Spain was persuaded to enter a secret agreement with France regarding Portugal. The Treaty of Fontainebleau, signed on October 27th, 1807, was concerned with Portugal and its partition. However, there was something more to this treaty. France needed to push Portugal into accepting its control, and the treaty permitted a French army of twenty-eight thousand men to cross Spain. A reserve of forty thousand troops at Bayonne was included in the event of English intervention. This meant that France could legally enter Spain. The French were successful in

---

[58] Britannica, T. E. (2024, April 30). Peninsular War. Retrieved from Britannica.com: https://www.britannica.com/event/Peninsular-War.

Portugal and forced the Portuguese royal family to seek asylum in Brazil. However, there were also French troops in northern Spain.[59]

The Spanish government was on the brink of collapse. Godoy could not organize any resistance to the French presence in northern Spain and wanted the king to seek refuge in Spanish America, but that did not happen. A rival faction in the Spanish court was able to have Godoy dismissed and forced Charles to abdicate. Charles IV's son was recognized as King Ferdinand VII on March 17th, 1808.[60]

Napoleon Intervenes

Napoleon was concerned that the chaos in the Spanish government might result in a political change that would make Spain more sympathetic to Great Britain. Rather than risk a potential enemy on his border, Napoleon decided to use the Treaty of Fontainebleau to invade Spain under the pretext of helping an ally. France invaded Spain on February 9th, 1808. On March 27th, Marshal Murat entered Madrid.

Portrait of Joseph Bonaparte.[xiii]

Ferdinand wanted Napoleon to confirm that he, Ferdinand, was the new king of Spain since his father wanted to protest the change. Napoleon convinced both to travel to Bayonne for a conference. Instead of a meeting, Napoleon pressured both into renouncing their respective claims to the throne on May 5th. Napoleon then appointed his brother, Joseph Bonaparte, as the new king of Spain.

Spanish Resistance

Napoleon underestimated the patriotism of the Spanish population. People in Madrid revolted on May 2nd, but the uprising was quickly suppressed. However, the Spanish resistance was not over. The Spanish

---

[59] Burkholder, S. H. (2024, June 10). Treaty of Fontainebleau (1807). Retrieved from Encyclopedia.com: https://www.encyclopedia.com/humanities/encyclopedias-almanacs-transcripts-and-maps/fontainebleau-treaty-1807.

[60] Britannica, T. E. Peninsular War.

fought back and forced the French to retreat. The French army was defeated at Baylen, which marked the first major defeat of Napoleon's army in a land battle. The Spanish success story continued, and they were able to force Joseph Bonaparte out of Madrid in August.

Napoleon decided to personally intervene in the situation. He led an army of approximately 300,000 men into Spain and crushed the Spanish resistance. One would think that would have settled the matter, but a new player was about to enter the game, and he would prove to be Napoleon's greatest nemesis.[61]

Sir Arthur Wellesley (Duke of Wellington)

Napoleon's battlefield success was due partly to the quality of the commanders he faced. Those generals were typically nothing special and rarely posed a threat to the French emperor. Napoleon's advantage in this arena would gradually erode as the performance of his enemies improved. The change started in the Peninsular War when a British general came into the picture.

Sir Arthur Wellesley was a career officer who served in Europe and India. He was particularly successful in battles on the Indian subcontinent and even developed some of the strategies that he would later use in the Napoleonic Wars there. His better qualities were common sense, attention to detail, care of his soldiers and their provisions, and maintaining good relations with civilians. He was also capable of making firm decisions at the right moment. He is commonly known as the Duke of Wellington, and his moniker was the Iron Duke. He became the worst nightmare the French ever had.[62]

The Duke of Wellington.

---

[61] Pisa, J. d. (2011, October 5). Napoleon's Nightmare: Guerilla Warfare in Spain (1808-1814). Retrieved from Smallwarsjournal.com: https://smallwarsjournal.com/jrnl/art/napoleon%c2%b4s-nightmare-guerrilla-warfare-in-spain-1808-1814.

[62] Jacques Godechot, E. P. (2024, April 30). Arthur Wellesley, 1st Duke of Wellington. Retrieved from Britannica.com: https://www.britannica.com/biography/Arthur-Wellesley-1st-Duke-of-

Great Britain decided to help the Portuguese and Spanish in their resistance against France. An expeditionary force of fourteen thousand men under Wellington, who at the time was a lieutenant general, landed in Portugal in August 1808.

Wellington wasted no time in taking the fight to the enemy. On August 17th, Wellington defeated the French at the Battle of Roliça and followed that up with a victory at Vimeiro on August 21st. He was clearly on the offensive, but Wellington was checkmated by his own commanders.

Wellington's supervisors negotiated the Convention of Cintra, which allowed the French to leave Portugal. There was an outpouring of public rage in Great Britain about this agreement, and Wellington had to return to Great Britain to face court-martial. Fortunately for Britain, he was acquitted.[63]

Wellington would later be reinstated, but in the meantime, the Peninsular War was entering a stage of immense tragedy for the Spanish people.

Unconventional Warfare

The Grande Armée was used to fighting conventional battles that followed certain rules. What happened in the Peninsular War was entirely different. The French were not always facing organized columns of soldiers. Instead, they had to deal with bands of guerrilla fighters who did not follow the conventions of civilized combat.

Guerrilla bands were formed not long after the French invasion. The French tried to quell these attacks, but it only resulted in the guerrilla bands getting larger. The guerrilla bands attacked those targets that had the best chance of disrupting French supply lines and gathering loot. The attacks on couriers forced the occupiers to provide military escorts for messengers.

Every retaliation served to stiffen the resistance of the Spanish. The French soldiers could not be sure if and when they were going to be attacked. More and more French troops had to be sent to Spain to fight. The civilian population of Spain suffered from the attacks and the

---

Wellington.

[63] National Army Museum. (2024, June 10). Peninsular War. Retrieved from Nam.ac.uk: https://www.nam.ac.uk/explore/peninsular-war.

retaliations, but they appeared united in their desire to rid the country of the French. So much time, effort, and resources were expended that Napoleon began to refer to the entire Iberian Peninsula as the "Spanish Ulcer."[64]

British Efforts

The conventional war between British and French soldiers continued, but the results were inconclusive. The British were forced to evacuate Spain at Corunna on January 16th, 1809, but they were not finished in the Iberian Peninsula. Wellington returned to the warfront in 1809 and was able to drive Field Marshal Jean-de-Dieu Soult out of Portugal. Wellington then moved into Spain and scored a victory at the Battle of Talavera. Wellington had to retreat because of logistical problems and because he needed to secure his supply lines. However, he demonstrated that the British were still in the conflict and that the French did not have absolute control over the peninsula.[65]

Wellington secured the position of the British army thanks to defensive fortifications he ordered to be constructed near Lisbon. The Lines of Torres Vedras were constructed between October 1809 and October 1810 and were a network of forts and redoubts with trenches and roads that extended for approximately fifty miles. It took advantage of the terrain around Lisbon region. When Marshal André Masséna tried to capture Lisbon with over sixty thousand men, he was effectively stopped by these defenses and had to fall back.

The Peninsular War continued, but there were no major developments during the following few years. Tens of thousands of French troops were tied down by activity in Spain and Portugal, depriving Napoleon of badly needed soldiers. The Peninsular War's manpower requirements would affect Napoleon's execution of what was not only his greatest military campaign but also the worst disaster of the Napoleonic Wars.

---

[64] Mark, H. W. (2023, August 7). Peninsular War. Retrieved from World History Encyclopedia: https://www.worldhistory.org/Peninsular_War/.

[65] Jacques Godechot, E. P. Arthur Wellesley, 1st Duke of Wellington.

Chapter 8: The Culture of the Time

Before we talk about the final major campaign of the Napoleonic Wars, let's take a look at the culture that blossomed. Wars are disruptive, but they do not force society to a dead stop. Creative people continue to paint, compose, and perform artistic works for the enjoyment and improvement of others. The Napoleonic Wars coincided with the Romantic movement. It was a time of creative experimentation and a move away from older music, art, and poetry styles.

There were giants of the arts during this time. They dared to challenge conventional practices and generated cultural masterpieces that are still enjoyed today. Let's examine several of these highly creative people and take note of how they improved society.

Characteristics of the Romantic Movement

Several popular themes can be found in the Romantic movement. The Romantics considered nature a source of inspiration and beauty. The Romantic movement also centered on the individual and personal expression. Introspective behavior and rebellious spirit were integral themes, as the main characters were often developed as being distant from society. Mythology and the supernatural could be found in various artistic works of this time as well.

The Romantic movement began before the Napoleonic Wars and continued long after the guns fell silent. Nevertheless, the wars sparked the creative forces that changed the cultural world. Emotion and passion replaced sedate parlor musings, and the vortex of war provided the energy to create astounding original pieces.

Music

The master of music in the Romantic movement was Ludwig van Beethoven. Earlier composers wrote works that were soft and gentle. Beethoven's music booms like an artillery barrage across a concert hall. His symphonies can start slow and smooth and end with a thunder blast of trumpets. Beethoven was already an established composer when the Napoleonic Wars began, and he would compose some of his greatest works during those years.

The Eroica Symphony

Beethoven initially was a fervent supporter of Napoleon because he believed that the French leader was an advocate for the ideals of the French Revolution. Symphony No. 3 was initially composed to honor Napoleon, but Beethoven was infuriated by Napoleon's coronation as emperor. So, he renamed the musical score the Eroica Symphony.

The symphony's title page with Napoleon's name erased.[iv]

This composition was a revolutionary piece. The work has more emotion than earlier writers, such as Mozart, would have used. Beethoven attempted to capture the mood of the time with dramatic and not sentimental music. It was a surprising break from tradition and was well received.

The Fifth Symphony

Beethoven wrote the Fifth Symphony between 1804 and 1808 when war was raging in central Europe and Napoleon was conducting decisive campaigns in Germany and Austria. This symphony also reflects the heightened energy of the Napoleonic years. Vienna was Beethoven's home at the time, and it was threatened by the French army. The bold character of the music is symbolic of the resolve of the Viennese in the face of an ominous threat.

The composer was disappointed with Napoleon and how the French leader had changed. However, this did not mean that Beethoven turned his back on the Bonaparte family. Beethoven's notoriety was so great and his music so splendid that Jerome Bonaparte, King of Westphalia, offered the composer the position of *kapellmeister* at the Westphalian court.

By 1814, Beethoven was a confirmed German nationalist and was opposed to Napoleon. He created a short orchestral work in celebration of Wellington's victory at Vitoria in 1813. Any illusions that Beethoven had about Napoleon being a champion of liberty were gone.[66]

There is a fascinating personal note to Beethoven's efforts during these years. The composer grew more and more deaf. He could not hear the music that he was creating, but it was still magnificent. How was it possible that a deaf man could write music that he could not even hear?

The answer is more intellectual than physical. The composer lost his hearing, but he did not lose his mind. Beethoven had been exposed to music since he was a toddler. Musical notes and the sounds of various instruments surrounded his days. He could no longer hear the sound, but Beethoven remembered how certain chords sounded. He used his memory to create some of the most incredible music we have ever heard.

Art: Getting the Message Out

The *Coronation of Napoleon* is a massive painting that is currently in the Louvre Museum. It shows Napoleon crowning his wife Josephine as various dignitaries, including the pope, are watching. In the stands above

---

[66] Lee, A. (2018, March 3). Beethoven and Napoleon. Retrieved from Historytoday.com: https://www.historytoday.com/archive/music-time/beethoven-and-napoleon.

Napoleon's mother, in the center of the painting, we see somebody who is busy sketching something on paper. That is the artist of the work, Jacques-Louis David.

Coronation of Napoleon *by Jacque-Louis David.*ⁿⁱ

David is an interesting person in art history. He was influenced by the neoclassicist style of painting and is famous for his *Oath of the Horatii* and the *Death of Socrates*.

He was a member of the Royal Academy and a favorite painter of the Bourbon aristocracy. That did not stop him from switching sides at the start of the French Revolution. David was a Jacobin who supported Robespierre. His work, the *Death of Marat*, was an icon of the French Revolution.

David was already an established artist at the time of the Napoleonic Wars, and he is technically not part of the Romantic movement. However, his role during the Napoleonic Wars was significant in the art world. David was Napoleon's personal artist.[67]

Artistic Propaganda

Napoleon recognized the value of propaganda and how crucial visual representation could be in shaping public opinion. David's representations of Napoleon, particularly the work *Napoleon Crossing the Alps*, depict the emperor as a heroic figure. Later works show

---

[67] The Open University. (2024, June 10). 3 Gros and the Napoleonic Propaganda Machine. Retrieved from Open.edu: https://www.open.edu/openlearn/history-the-arts/history-art/napoleonic-paintings/content-section-3.1

Napoleon with a crown of golden laurels, connecting him to the classical rulers of Rome. Interestingly, while David was an ardent revolutionary during the French Revolution, he quickly transferred his allegiance to the French Empire. Perhaps the painter was as much a businessman as he was an artist. He knew where his commissions were, and he gravitated toward the money.[68]

Painting the Nightmare

Francisco Goya's artistic career before Napoleon came to power was comparable to David's. He was a court painter for the Spanish Bourbons and painted beautiful pictures of the Spanish royalty and the aristocracy. His life did not seem to have any ripples in the water, but the Spanish invasion of 1808 changed Goya's perspective dramatically.

Goya saw the devastation of war, and he could not turn away. His work *The Second of May 1808* depicts the street fighting that occurred in Madrid when the population rose in revolt. A second painting, *Third of May 1808*, is a depiction of when the French executed Spanish insurgents to suppress the uprising. Goya's message to the viewer in both works was an antiwar statement that showed the violence and inhumanity of war.

Second of May 1808.[xvii]

---

[68] The Clark. (2024, June 10). David & Napoleon. Retrieved from Clarkart.edu: https://www.clarkart.edu/microsites/jacques-louis-david/david-napoleon.

Goya did not hesitate to depict the horror of warfare. He departed from the royal court's urbane sensitivities to show the brutal aspects of revolt and depression. Human suffering was a theme that the Spanish painter concentrated on.

The Disasters of War

The most significant contribution Goya made to the art world was *The Disasters of War* series. This was a collection of eighty-two etchings Goya created between 1810 and 1820.

The first forty-seven etchings concentrate on episodes during the Peninsular War and the consequences of the fighting. Plates 48 to 64 are a record of the Madrid famine of 1811-1812. The final group of etchings depicts his disappointment in the Bourbon restoration, which opposed all the state and religious reforms that had taken place in the prior years.

Goya challenged the viewer to confront the realities of war and not be seduced by glamorous depictions of valor. One can see starvation, humiliation, atrocity, and inhumanity in *The Disasters of War*. He did not use his art as a means of propaganda but as a way to send a message that war was not the answer.[69]

A Spanish civilian about to decapitate a French soldier.[xviii]

---

[69] Franciscogoya.com. (2024, June 10). The Disaster of War, 1810-1820 by Francisco Goya. Retrieved from Franciscogoya.com: https://www.franciscogoya.com/disasters-of-war.jsp.

The prints were so dramatic and overwhelming that they were not published until 1863.

Francisco Goya is remembered primarily for the works he created during the Peninsular War. A later artist who was greatly influenced by Goya's work was another Spaniard, Pablo Picasso. Picasso shared Goya's indignation at inhumanity and respected the earlier artist's freedom of tone and creation. While Picasso studied the works of other Spanish artists, he was so inspired by Goya's work that he was given the nickname "Little Goya."[70]

The Disasters of War had an effect on Pablo Picasso. The stark scenes that Goya depicted inspired Picasso to create his masterpiece, *Guernica*, which was another plea to bring an end to violence.

The Poet's Quill

War was the most important fact of British life from 1793 to 1815, and it became the principal poetic subject, according to Betty T. Bennett, a distinguished professor of literature.[71] Great Britain did not suffer material damage comparable to Spain or Germany, but the war affected the psyche of the British people. A sense of disillusionment, a feeling that the revolutionary ideals of the late 18th century would never materialize or that war could be dignified, crept into the spirit of the British.

William Wordsworth created some of his best works before the Napoleonic Wars started, but he did compose poems during the war years. His work, *Elegiac Stanzas*, was composed in 1805 in memory of his brother who drowned in a shipwreck. It speaks of the loss and mourning that were prevalent in a society that had to accept the loss of young men to war. It also shows the fragility of life and the unpredictability of life's twists and turns.

Wordsworth used the Romantic movement's theme of nature as a place for consolation. However, a sense of grief permeates the lines of his poem:

---

[70] Musee Goya Castres. (2024, June 10). Goya-Picasso: A Cross-View. Retrieved from museegoya.fr: https://www.museegoya.fr/en/goya-in-piccaso-s-eye.

[71] Bainbridge, S. (2016, June 2). Romanticism and War. Retrieved from Oxford Academic: https://academic.oup.com/edited-volume/43514/chapter/364255284?login=false.

"I have submitted to a new control:

a power is gone, which nothing can restore;

a deep distress hath humanized my Soul."[72]

A Disillusioned Pilgrim

The Grand Tour of Europe was once part of the education of a young English aristocrat. The Napoleonic Wars prevented that, but Lord Byron still traveled through Spain and Portugal. He was shocked at the devastation he saw, and the poet rebelled against any romantic notions of heroism that people had. His work, *Childe Harold's Pilgrimage*, part of which was published in 1812, evoked a revulsion to what war was like. Canto I contains particularly sharp lines.

"Let their bleached bones,

and blood's un-bleaching stain,

long marked the battle-field with hideous awe: thus, only

May our sons conceived the scenes we saw."[73]

The great British victory at the Battle of Waterloo did not impress Lord Byron at all. In a later work, *Don Juan*, Byron attacks the Duke of Wellington:

"And I would be delighted to learn who,

Save you and yours, have gained by Waterloo?"[74]

National identity was also a theme used by poets during the Napoleonic Wars. The Italian poet Ugo Foscolo's *Dei Sepolcri* is concerned with national identity and cultural ties to the past. The poet saw the St. Cloud Decree as an insult to Italian culture because it regulated burial practices in Italy. Foscolo believed that tombs and monuments of the dead could inspire the living and remind people of their country's glorious past.

---

[72] Wordsworth, W. (2024, June 19). Elegias Stanzas Suggested by a Picture of Peele Castle in a Storm, Painted by Sir George Beaumont. Retrieved from Poetryfoundation.org: https://www.poetryfoundation.org/poems/45516/elegiac-stanzas-suggested-by-a-picture-of-peele-castle-in-a-storm-painted-by-sir-george-beaumont.

[73] Lord Byron. The Works of Lord Byron Vol. 2. https://genius.com/Lord-byron-the-works-of-lord-byron-vol-2-to-inez-annotated.

[74] Collinson, A. (2015, May 11). In Literature and Song: The Legacy of the Napoleonic Wars. Retrieved from Ageofrevolution.org: https://ageofrevolution.org/in-literature-and-song-the-legacy-of-the-napoleonic-wars/.

"Only those who leave no legacy of affection
find little joy in their earn; and if they gaze
after their obsequies, they see their spirit wander
among the laments of Achaean temples,
of a thousand
desolate Greek shades."[75]

Foscolo took a risky step in this poem and criticized the French emperor:

"And you, Hector, will be honored in tears,
were holy and lamented is the blood
shed for one's country, and as long as the Sun
shines upon human suffering."[76]

<u>Deal with the Devil</u>

Johann Wolfgang von Goethe is one of the giants of the modern literary world. His epic work *Faust* was published in two parts; the first was made public in 1808. Although the author does not directly confront the Napoleonic Wars, *Faust I* is interwoven with character references that mirrored current events.

The main character, Dr. Heinrich Faust, makes a deal with the devil, giving his soul in return for unlimited knowledge, power, and pleasure. Faust has enormous ambition, similar to what Goethe perceived in Napoleon. Goethe believed that Napoleon's genius bordered on demonic. Faust's desire to satisfy personal ambitions reflects the changes brought about by Napoleon. What is interesting to notice is the respect that Napoleon had for Goethe. He tried to persuade Goethe to relocate to Paris, but the author politely declined the invitation.[77]

The culture of the Napoleonic Wars suggests a growing fatigue settled in Europe. The hopes for positive change slowly crumbled, as reality and the tumult of war made people more cynical. The conflicts kept dragging

---

[75] Foscolo, U. (2024, June 11). Ugo Foscolo-Opere Omnia. Retrieved from Foscolo.letteraturaoperaomnia.org:
https://foscolo.letteraturaoperaomnia.org/foscolo_dei_sepolcri.html.

[76] Foscolo, U. Ugo Foscolo-Opere Omnia.

[77] Keene, R. (2024, June 10). Napoleon and Goethe: Touchstone of Genius. Retrieved from Thearticle.com: https://www.thearticle.com/napoleon-and-goethe-touchstone-of-genius.

on, and only a few months of tranquility separated one war from another. A cataclysmic event was forming, and it would become real in 1812.

Chapter 9: The Invasion of Russia: Napoleon's Catastrophic Campaign

The Continental System was a bad public policy that was riddled with holes. It was almost impossible for France to enforce the rules, given the expansive coastline of Europe. Nevertheless, Napoleon was committed to it. The obsession to bring Great Britain to its knees through economic pressure resulted in the Peninsular War, which would cause other problems for the French emperor. His determination to uphold the Continental System eventually led to his greatest mistake.

War of the Fifth Coalition

France was the dominant power in Europe in January 1809. France's control over the continent was nearly complete despite the distractions of the Peninsular War. Austria had already been humiliated by Napoleon and lost considerable amounts of territory. The Habsburgs wanted to regain some of their foreign possessions. The Austrian army had been reformed, and the government was willing to take a chance.

Consequently, Emperor Francis I ordered the Austrians to invade Bavaria on April 10th, 1809. It was a mistake because Bavaria was an ally of France, and Napoleon was obligated to come to its defense. This began the War of the Fifth Coalition.

Austria hoped that Prussia would help, but the Prussian army was too small and was unwilling to risk a defeat. Great Britain sent financial subsidies to Austria, but it was clear that the main force confronting Napoleon would be Austria this time around.

Changes to the Army

The Austrians had worked to modernize their army. Archduke Charles, commander in chief of the Austrian military, introduced several reforms. These included reorganizing the army into lines and reserve corps that resembled Napoleon's organization of troops. Additionally, Charles introduced mass conscription that supplied fresh troops. Austria was able to field the largest army it had ever seen.

Fighting against Napoleon was a gamble that Emperor Francis I was willing to take. The Peninsular War caused the French to direct hundreds of thousands of soldiers to the Iberian Peninsula. It appeared that the odds were slightly in favor of the Austrians.

However, Napoleon was aware of the Austrian buildup and prepared for the possibility of war. He ordered a counterattack after the Austrians invaded Bavaria. After several battles, the French met the Austrians at Eckmuuhl on April 22nd, 1809. The Austrians were doing a better job of fighting than before, although they lost that battle thanks to Napoleon arriving just in time. Napoleon captured Vienna on May 13th, but the Austrian army was still in the field and, while bloodied, could fight on.

A Rude Surprise

Napoleon wanted to finish off the Austrian army that Archduke Charles was leading, so he marched the French army out of Vienna to find it. The retreating Austrians had destroyed the Danube's bridges. Napoleon was forced to move downstream and build a pontoon bridge to the island of Lobau on May 20th. Another bridge was constructed from that island to the other side of the Danube, and French troops moved across and occupied Aspern and Essling.

Archduke Charles did not contest the crossing. He wanted to attack part of the French army that crossed over and defeat it before the rest could come to its rescue. The Austrians attacked on May 21st, and the French were able to beat them back. Archduke Charles resumed the offensive on May 22nd. An attack by the Austrian reserve, led by Archduke Charles himself, got on the left side of the French and forced Napoleon to retreat to a defensive position. The Battle of Aspern-Essling ended in Napoleon's defeat.

The victory was a significant boost to Austrian morale. Unfortunately, Archduke Charles did not follow up on the success. Napoleon would strike back a few weeks later.[78]

Wagram

The French and Austrian armies were now on opposite sides of the Danube. Napoleon would not concede and began to gather more troops for a second attempt to destroy the Austrian army. It took several weeks, but by the beginning of July, he had nearly 170,000 soldiers and 600 artillery pieces ready. The Austrians were able to assemble 140,000 men and 400 cannons. The French started to cross the river on July 4th, 1809.

The Battle of Wagram commenced on July 5th. There was heavy fighting, and the French made some gains, but the Austrians were in defensive positions that could not be breached. Both sides suffered heavy casualties on the first day.

Napoleon gave a demonstration of shock and awe on July 6th. His artillery was positioned in grand batteries, and the engagement started with an enormous artillery duel in which more than one thousand cannons opened fire on each other. This was followed by a massive coordinated attack by the French, with Marshal Davout attacking the left wing of the Austrians and Marshal Masséna targeting the right.

A central assault by the French broke through the Austrian lines, while, at the same time, French cavalry charged into the Austrian reserves. Under enormous pressure from the advancing enemy, Archduke Charles ordered a retreat.

Wagram was an enormous battle in which 300,000 troops fought each other. It is also noted for the use of massed artillery that resulted in a total of nearly seventy-seven thousand casualties. The losses seriously weakened Napoleon's army, but the Austrians could not press further. Peace negotiations between Austria and France started, resulting in the Treaty of Schönbrunn, signed on October 14th, 1809.[79]

The treaty was an embarrassment for Austria. Additional territory was carved out of the Austrian Empire and given to France and French allies.

---

[78] Hickman, K. (2015, March 10). Napoleonic Wars: Battle of Aspern-Essling. Retrieved from Thoughtco.com: https://www.thoughtco.com/napoleonic-battle-of-aspern-essling-2361108.

[79] Frithowulf, H. (2024, February 29). Battle of Wagram: Napoleon's Masterstroke. Retrieved from Malevus.com: https://malevus.com/battle-of-wagram/.

Joseph Bonaparte was formally recognized as the king of Spain, and Austria was forced to pay a large indemnity. Moreover, the Austrian army was reduced to 150,000 men, and Austria was to become part of the Continental System. One Austrian concession was more personal, though.[80]

The Divorce

Napoleon's relationship with his wife Josephine was complex. Both were unfaithful, but Napoleon was deeply in love with his wife. The main problem was that Josephine could not produce an heir. By 1809, she was past her childbearing years. Napoleon needed a male successor to continue his dynasty. Josephine could no longer fulfill that need for him.

Napoleon formally divorced Josephine on December 15th, 1809. He made it clear that the divorce was necessary for the good of France. He was generous and permitted his former wife to keep her title as empress. She was given a residence at Château de Malmaison and a substantial financial settlement. Both maintained a friendly relationship despite the divorce.

The Austrian Marriage

The Habsburgs had a reputation for using marriages as a diplomatic tool. They saw an opportunity to gain better relations with France by marrying Napoleon to Emperor Francis I's daughter, Marie Louise. Negotiations between France and Austria began in January 1810. A marriage contract was agreed upon on March 9th, 1810, and Marie Louise married Napoleon by proxy on March 11th, 1810. A civil marriage occurred on April 1st, 1810, when Marie Louise arrived in France, and a religious ceremony was held on April 2nd.[81]

Marie Louise was very young (she was eighteen years old at the time of the marriage), but she understood her duty. On March 20th, 1811, she gave birth to a healthy boy who was named after his father. Napoleon now had the heir he had so desperately wanted.

---

[80] Britannica, T. E. (2024, June 11). Treaty of Schonbrunn. Retrieved from Britannica.com: https://www.britannica.com/event/Treaty-of-Schonbrunn.

[81] Napoleon.org. (2010, March). The Marriage of Napoleon I and Marie-Louise of Austria. Retrieved from Napoleon.org: https://www.napoleon.org/en/history-of-the-two-empires/timelines/the-marriage-of-napoleon-i-and-marie-louise-of-austria/.

Empress Marie Louise with her son, who was given the title "King of Rome." Portrait by Jacques Franque.[xix]

Eyes on Russia

Napoleon was the master of Europe, and Great Britain was the only nation strong enough to continue fighting him. Nevertheless, the French emperor was tired of fighting coalition wars. He successfully reduced the military power of Prussia and Austria, but there was one final country that could field a sizable army against him: Russia. Napoleon needed to neutralize any potential threat from the east and bind the Russian Empire closer to France.

However, Russia was not cooperating. It had agreed to be a part of the Continental System, but those trade restrictions hurt the Russian economy. Tsar Alexander turned a blind eye to the violations, allowing Russians to blatantly trade with Great Britain. Despite declarations of friendship, Napoleon and Tsar Alexander did not trust each other.

Napoleon continued to worry that Russia would eventually disregard the Treaty of Tilsit and become an ally of France's enemies. Bonaparte finally concluded that a preemptive strike of massive proportions would be the best way to put Russia back in line.

A Massive Force

Napoleon organized one of the largest military forces in European history to teach Russia a lesson. He gathered an army of nearly 600,000 men from all parts of the French Empire, including France, Italy, Poland, and his German allies. His invasion force was divided into three primary groups.

- The Northern Army Group would be under the command of Marshal Étienne Macdonald and would concentrate on the Baltic region.
- The Central Army Group was under Napoleon's direct command, and its target was Moscow.
- The Southern Army Group was commanded by Karl Philipp, Prince of Schwarzenberg, and was assigned to secure the southern flank from any Russian attack.

An immediate challenge for this military force was language barriers. The logistical planning for the invasion was staggering.

The invasion of Russia would be greater than any of the previous campaigns of the Napoleonic Wars. Feeding and supplying the troops was a monumental task. The French had 20 train battalions, with 7,848 carriages and wagons tasked with providing 40 days' worth of supplies for the army. In addition, auxiliary supply convoys were created to carry enough medical supplies, flour, and bread to supply 300,000 men for 2 months.

Supply depots were established at Danzig, Magdeburg, and Breslow. The Central Army Group had sufficient provisions for the Northern and Southern groups and confronted supply problems brought on by prioritizing supplies for the Central Group and Russian raids.[82]

The Grande Armée crossed the Niemen River on June 24th, 1812. Napoleon expected a relatively short campaign, and the initial stages of the invasion went smoothly.

---

[82] Thenapoleonicwars.net. (2024, June 11). Napoleon's Invasion of Russia. Retrieved from Thenapoleonicwars.net: https://www.thenapoleonicwars.net/invasion-of-russia.

Napoleon also anticipated an immediate confrontation with the Russian army. He was disappointed.

Challenges of Fighting in Russia

Napoleon grossly underestimated the size of Russia. The nation was vast, stretching for thousands of miles. The French also discovered that the road system was so primitive that a storm could turn the road into a muddy swamp in minutes. Alexander had ordered a scorched earth policy, and where there once had been acres of wheat flowing in the breeze was nothing but burned stalks.

Bonaparte had hoped one or two significant battles would determine the outcome. In his defense, that happened in the other coalition wars; a major engagement would result in a smashing victory, and peace negotiations would commence. Tsar Alexander did not play by Napoleon's rules. Instead, the Russians kept moving back, denying the enemy an opportunity to fight.[83]

Napoleon was aware of what the enemy was doing, but he continued to advance. He hoped that by capturing Moscow, he could convince Alexander to enter peace negotiations. It was a mistaken assumption. Alexander had matured since the defeat at Austerlitz. This time, he listened carefully to his commanders in the field and agreed with the strategy of retreating. The supply lines of the French were being stretched to the limit, and Russian attacks on the columns were wearing down the invaders' morale.

Finally, there was a battle between the French and the Russians. It took place at Smolensk from August 16th to the 18th. What was notable about this encounter was the French artillery bombardment of the city. Approximately 84 percent of the buildings were destroyed, and only one thousand inhabitants remained. The retreat strategy had now run its course. The Russians began to organize to resist the French in a pitched battle.[84]

---

[83] Historyskills.com. (2024, June 11). Napoleon's Catastrophic Invasion of Russia: A Military Miscalculation of Epic Proportions. Retrieved from Historyskills.com: https://www.historyskills.com/classroom/modern-history/napoleon-s-russian-invasion/.

[84] DetailedPedia.com. (2024, June 11). Battle of Smolensk (1812). Retrieved from Detailedpedia.com: https://www.detailedpedia.com/wiki-Battle_of_Smolensk_%281812%29.

Borodino

Borodino is approximately eighty miles west of Moscow. The area has natural defensive features, including a river and, more importantly, ridges that could be fortified. The Russian commander, Marshal Mikhail Kutuzov, chose this as the place to make their stand.

Several fortifications were constructed to strengthen the Russian defensive line. The Raevsky redoubt, placed in the center, and the Bagration flèches at the southern end of the Russian line were the most prominent. The artillery reinforced the defense, and the Russians had more than six hundred cannons.

The French arrived at the battlefield, which began on September 7th. French artillery bombarded the Russian positions and created significant gaps. A major French attack occurred on the Bagration flèches, but the fiercest fighting occurred at the Raevsky redoubt. The redoubt changed hands numerous times during the battle.

Both sides had attacks and counterattacks. Historians have criticized Napoleon for not sending in his Imperial Guard despite being begged to do so by his marshals. His reluctance permitted the Russians to stiffen their lines. The fighting got more intense, and both sides took heavy casualties. The Raevsky redoubt was finally captured, and the Russians retreated. The battle was technically over.

The Battle of Moscow by Louis-François, Baron Lejeune.”

September 7th, 1812, was the bloodiest day of all the Napoleonic Wars. Both sides were too exhausted by the end of the day to continue the fighting. Napoleon had tactically won the battle, but the Russian army was able to retreat in good order. They would fight another day.

Napoleon and his army achieved a primary military objective on September 14th, for that was the day when the French entered Moscow. Napoleon wanted the city, and it cost him thousands of veterans to obtain it. He entered the city and received a major surprise.

Moscow was abandoned.

The citizens had fled the city. Napoleon quickly discovered that the Russian scorched earth policy did not just apply to wheatfields. Arsonists set fire to Moscow starting on the night of September 14th. Within a few days, Napoleon was in control of a burned-out city.

Attempts were made to reach the tsar to start peace negotiations, but Alexander was uninterested. Napoleon waited several weeks, but there was no response from St. Petersburg. Supplies were beginning to run short, and the French emperor realized he had to evacuate the city. On October 19th, 1812, the Grande Armée marched out of Moscow. It would face a determined Russian army with an ally that even Napoleon could not defeat.

The Russians harassed the retreating French army. Napoleon intended to lead his troops over the ground that had not been devastated by the war. Kutuzov was not going to let that happen. On October 24th, 1812, the Russians engaged the French in the town of Maloyaroslavets. The French won, but the Russians retreated toward Kaluga and blocked Napoleon's intended route. The French had to retreat northwest through Smolensk, which meant that Napoleon was moving over the route they had used to approach Moscow. The land had already been devastated, making living off the land difficult.

<u>General Winter</u>

Russia has long relied on the weather to help repel invasions. King Charles XII of Sweden learned that in the 18th century. Hitler would discover what a menace General Winter would be in the 20th century. The first snowstorm the French endured occurred on November 6th, 1812, and it would not be the last.

The winter weather was brutal. Temperatures fell as low as -22°F, and the soldiers suffered from frostbite because they had not been issued winter clothing. The horses also suffered because they did not have horseshoes suitable for the ice and snow. The French had already suffered a large number of casualties from the battles, and now the Grande Armée was losing men to starvation and hypothermia. And still, the Russians kept harassing them.[85]

A depiction of what the French forces faced during the harsh Russian winter.[xxi]

Crossing the Berezina River

The Grande Armée still trudged on despite the terrible conditions. The Berezina River blocked the western progress, and the army was required to cross it. The Russians had already moved ahead and captured the bridge spanning the river and destroyed it once they gained control of the west bank on November 23rd, 1812. The French built two pontoon bridges despite being under heavy attack. They crossed the river from November 26th to the 29th, but they lost thousands of men in the process and most of the army's baggage.

Napoleon Leaves

All was not well back in Paris. General Claude François de Malet spread a rumor that Napoleon was dead and attempted a coup d'état on October 23rd. It was unsuccessful, and the general was executed, but

---

[85] Napoleon.org. (2024, June 11). Napoleon's Russian Campaign: The Retreat. Retrieved from Napoleon.org: https://www.napoleon.org/en/history-of-the-two-empires/timelines/napoleons-russian-campaign-the-retreat/.

Napoleon was greatly disturbed when the news reached him. He was so worried that this would not be the only attempt to overthrow him that he decided to return to France. He set out for Paris on December 5th and was in the French capital before Christmas.

Meanwhile, the French army entered Vilna under the command of Marshal Murat. The soldiers' morale was extremely low because of Napoleon's departure, and there was worse to come. The army experienced an outbreak of typhus that killed thousands of men. Murat decided to leave Vilna. On December 12th, Kutuzov and his troops marched into the city. The last French soldiers crossed the Nieman River and left Russia behind on December 14th, 1812. The campaign was over.

The retreat would have been worse had it not been for the efforts of Marshal Ney. He was in charge of the rearguard, and he fought off attacks by Russians and Cossack partisans every step of the way out. His last action was at the Nieman River, guarding what was left of the army from the final assaults. Ney's stubborn courage and command of soldiers under horrible circumstances solidified his reputation as one of France's best marshals during the Napoleonic Wars.

<u>The Butcher's Bill</u>

The casualty figures of the Russian campaign were grim. Approximately 563,000 men were killed, wounded, or missing by the time the French forces left Russia. In addition, nearly 200,000 horses and more than 1,000 artillery pieces were lost in the effort.[86]

The Russian campaign was an unprecedented disaster. The French were accustomed to winning great victories and wars. Now, their military ranks were devastated. In addition, French allies lost men in a campaign that was a hopeless venture. Other European countries noticed the decline of France.

Prussia and Austria were still smarting from past humiliations. A defeated Napoleon presented a possible opportunity to regain lost territories and prestige. Great Britain was willing to provide financial support, and the Russians were in high spirits because of their victory. What was once considered impossible, that Napoleon could be brought

---

[86] New World Encyclopedia. (2024, June 11). French Invasion of Russia. Retrieved from New World Encyclopedia.com:
https://www.newworldencyclopedia.org/entry/French_invasion_of_Russia#Retreat_and_losses.

down, was beginning to look possible. The year 1813 was going to be a challenging one for Bonaparte.

Chapter 10: The War of the Sixth Coalition and the Abdication

France was left staggering after the Russian disaster. Approximately 300,000 French soldiers, including many seasoned veterans, died in the campaign. The Continental System was a complete failure, and France was experiencing economic problems brought on by the war and the constraints on markets. The most significant result of the Russian campaign was the damage to Napoleon's image. The French emperor was no longer invincible; he was vulnerable and human. A mystique that served his purposes for years vanished, and it did not go unnoticed in the other countries on the Continent.

The former enemies of France saw that the country was now crippled. The French Empire and its satellite states were shaken to the core. Ministers in various capitals were starting to wonder if there might be a way to end the Napoleonic era and the wars that resulted from it.

Prussia and Austria were technically allies of France, but they were looking for revenge and the possible return of lost territory. Russia had paid a price for its victory in 1812, but national pride and morale were incredibly high. The Russian army knew it could beat Napoleon, and it was hoping for more opportunities to do so. Great Britain relished the idea of finally ending a problem it had faced for years. It would take some sophisticated diplomacy and maneuvering to bring about another coalition.

Enter Metternich

Prince Klemens von Metternich was Austria's foreign minister and perhaps the most talented diplomat of his time. He was a conservative who hoped to restore stability to Europe.

Metternich did not necessarily want to return to the status quo, though. The old regimes of the 18th century could not be fully restored; revolutionary ideas were now laws. What the Austrian prince wanted was a balance of power in Europe. One nation should not be dictating terms to everyone else. Instead, balancing one power against another would make negotiating more acceptable than war.

Realignment

Prussia was required to provide troops for the Russian campaign. After Napoleon's defeat, the Russian army marched into Prussia and captured Königsberg on January 4th, 1813. Before this, the commander of the Prussian contingent, Lieutenant General Johann Yorck von Wartenburg, signed an armistice with the Russians on December 31st, 1812. King Frederick William III of Prussia initially denounced the armistice, but there was a wave of public enthusiasm in favor of renouncing all ties with France.

Frederick William III decided not to go against popular sentiment, and on February 28th, 1813, he signed the Treaty of Kalisz with the Russians. This treaty stipulated that Prussia and Russia were in an alliance, and neither would negotiate with Napoleon independently of the other. Together, Russia and Prussia invaded Saxony in March 1813.

Austria's alliance with France formally ended in February 1813, and the nation took a stance of armed neutrality. Austria was initially reluctant to enter any coalition against Napoleon. This hesitancy was understandable, given Austria's recent history of losing to the French.

Great Britain sought any chance to eliminate Napoleon, so it actively recruited allies. It persuaded Sweden to enter a military alliance on March 3rd, 1813, and the two nations formally declared war against France.

The genesis of a new coalition was beginning to take shape. Russia formally declared war against France on March 13th. Great Britain was willing to provide financial subsidies, and that financial assistance was slowly changing people's minds about entering a new war.

Napoleon on the Offensive

Napoleon was not napping while all this was going on. At the start of 1813, he realized he needed an almost complete overhaul of the French army and went to work to bring the troop level back to a normal size. On January 11th, 1813, Napoleon called up the conscription class that should have been summoned in 1814 as a contingent numbering 150,000 men and raised an additional 100,000 men from earlier conscription classes. He withdrew troops from Spain, although he left 150,000 soldiers on the peninsula. Extra troops were also raised, but these were inexperienced soldiers who needed training. The veterans who had been counted on in the past were now buried under the snow in Russia. Nevertheless, by April 15th, 1813, Napoleon had 226,000 soldiers under his command and marched out of Paris, heading toward Germany.

Metternich tried to broker a peace and met with Napoleon in April 1813. The Austrian diplomat asked Napoleon to return Illyria to the Austrian Empire, partition the Grand Duchy of Warsaw, and dissolve the Confederation of the Rhine. Metternich warned Napoleon that Austria would intervene against the side that did not agree with these proposals. Napoleon rejected the terms.

Napoleon left his wife as acting regent in Paris and took command of his Army of the Main. He crossed the Saale River on May 1st, 1813, and moved to aid Saxony. He confronted the Russian-Prussian army at Lützen on May 2nd and again from May 20th to the 21st at Bautzen. Both battles resulted in French victories.

These military successes once again demonstrated Napoleon Bonaparte's military acumen. He was not leading an army of battle-hardened veterans as in earlier campaigns, but he was still able to win. Moreover, he was taking the fight to the enemy, and by the end of the month, the coalition forces wanted an armistice. Napoleon agreed to pause the fighting, and the Plaaswitz Armistice, signed on June 4th, provided a temporary peace that would last until August 18th, 1813.[87]

Metternich the Mediator

Metternich continued his role as a peace broker and met with Napoleon on June 26th in Dresden. Metternich informed Bonaparte of the pending conditions and warned that Austria would join the coalition

---

[87] Mark, H. W. (2023, September 4). War of the Sixth Coalition. Retrieved from World History Encyclopedia: https://www.worldhistory.org/War_of_the_Sixth_Coalition/.

if those conditions were not accepted. The terms included the following:
- France surrendering the Illyrian Provinces to Austria
- France recognizing the independence of the Confederation of the Rhine
- The removal of all French troops from Germany and Italy
- France abandoning the Grand Duchy of Warsaw
- France restoring independence to Hesse-Kassel, Hanover, and the free cities of Hamburg and Lübeck
- The return of the Papal States, Piedmont, and all German possessions of the House of Orange to previous owners
- France restoring the 1806 borders to Prussia

This meeting took place at the wrong time for Metternich. Napoleon had previously won battles against the coalition and was confident of further military success. The emperor rejected the conditions outright.

In retrospect, those conditions were a little bit cynical. Metternich probably knew that France would reject them and that hostilities would continue with Austria fighting on the side of the new alliance. The situation was one of 19th-century realpolitik. Austria had been France's ally in 1812. By 1813, the situation had changed dramatically, and Metternich saw the possibility of regaining land and reputation while buying some time for Austria to rearm.[88]

The Treaties of Reichenbach

June 1813 saw other significant diplomatic movements. On June 14th, 1813, Great Britain signed a treaty with Prussia, agreeing to provide a financial subsidy of £666,666 to Prussia. The following day, Great Britain signed another treaty with Russia, which promised a subsidy of £1,333,334. The money promised would fund 80,000 Prussian soldiers and 160,000 Russian soldiers. A final treaty was signed on June 27th, 1813. This time, it was between Prussia, Russia, and Austria. Austria agreed to formally enter the war against Napoleon.

---

[88] Cheikh, M. (2020, September 24). Were Metternich's Peace Ouvertures in 1813 Genuine? Retrieved from Thenapoleonicwars.net:
https://www.thenapoleonicwars.net/forum/napoleon/were-metternich-s-peace-ouvertures-in-1813-genuine.

The members of the Sixth Coalition met at Trachtenberg on July 2nd to prepare a war strategy. It was decided that half a million men would be deployed in three army groups to oppose Napoleon. These were not divided by nationality; each army would be multinational, assuring that there would be cooperation between the member nations.

The plan was a departure from the standard way of dealing with Napoleon. Confrontation with Bonaparte was to be avoided. The Sixth Coalition would concentrate on defeating the French marshals instead. There would be better coordination between the allies than before, and the supply lines of the French army would be disrupted whenever possible.

Crown Prince Charles John of Sweden was the Trachtenberg Plan's principal architect. He was formally known as Jean-Baptiste Bernadotte and had once been one of Napoleon's most reliable marshals. The crown prince was now a principal advisor to the coalition and understood Napoleon's strategies and his frame of mind. Charles John would be invaluable in the months to come.

Portrait of Charles XIV John after he became king of Sweden and Norway.[xxii]

The Prague Congress

As a final effort to mediate peace, the Prague Peace Congress met in July and August, but nothing came of it. The armistice expired, and fighting began again. The coalition's plan of action was working, and French Marshal Nicolas Oudinot was beaten on August 23rd at Grossbeeren, and Marshal Macdonald was defeated at Katzbach on August 27th.

Dresden was a major supply depot in base operations for Napoleon's army. The coalition wanted to capture it, but Napoleon found out what the coalition planned to do and quickly moved reinforcements to Dresden, starting the march on August 23rd. His army was able to cover 120 miles in only four days.

Napoleon engaged with the Sixth Coalition from August 26th to the 27th in the Battle of Dresden. The weather conditions were terrible, and Napoleon used artillery to force the coalition armies to leave the battlefield. It was technically a victory for Napoleon, but he could not follow up on the success, and the coalition forces were able to retreat in good order.[89]

The Battle of Leipzig

The Battle of Leipzig is also known as the Battle of Nations and was fought from October 16th to October 19th, 1813. This was the most pivotal battle of the War of the Sixth Coalition.

The Sixth Coalition armies were able to coordinate their activity, and they attacked in multiple directions. The military force was close to 380,000 men, which outnumbered the 225,000 French troops. The battle line stretched between twelve and twenty-five miles, and over two thousand artillery pieces were deployed by the fighting armies.

The Sixth Coalition gradually encircled the French army and applied pressure on all sides. Napoleon took a central position, allowing his army to respond more effectively to attacks. The French emperor ordered several counterattacks to try to break out of the encirclement, and he fortified positions around Leipzig, which slowed down the coalition's movements.

The decisive moment came on October 18th. The Saxon troops fighting for the French defected. They went over to the coalition, which damaged the morale of the French forces. Fresh reinforcements strengthened the Sixth Coalition and allowed them to pressure the French lines significantly.

The French were forced to retreat on October 19th, and a premature explosion intended to destroy the only bridge over the Elster River caused the death of thousands of French and the capture of thirty thousand French soldiers. What was left of the Grande Armée finally made it across the river and were in full retreat toward the Rhine.

Leipzig was the bloodiest battle fought in the Napoleonic Wars. There were somewhere between 80,000 and 110,000 casualties. The French lost 325 artillery pieces, and over fifty generals were among the casualties.

---

[89] Britannica, T. E. (2024, May 14). Battle of Dresden. Retrieved from Britannica.com: https://www.britannica.com/event/Battle-of-Dresden.

The Battle of Leipzig by Vladimir Moshkov.[xxiii]

Napoleon was finished in Germany. His allies were beginning to desert him, and his enemies were now unified in using a well-thought-out plan to defeat him. The worst was yet to come.

Invasion of France, 1814

While things were falling apart in Germany, the Peninsular War became a disaster. The Duke of Wellington won the Battle of Vitoria on June 21st, 1813, and following that success, Madrid was taken. The French retreated north toward the Pyrenees with the British in pursuit. The last French stronghold in Spain, San Sebastian, fell in September 1813. Wellington then crossed the Pyrenees. His army was now in southern France.

The French opposition to the Sixth Coalition was falling like a house of cards. Napoleon achieved some victories, most notably during a six-day campaign in February 1814, but these achievements were little more than delaying actions. The Sixth Coalition armies entered Paris on March 31st, 1814. Although Napoleon wanted to continue, his marshals knew victory would be impossible. The only honorable thing for the French emperor to do was to abdicate. On April 6th, 1814, Napoleon gave in to the coalition's demand for an unconditional abdication. The Treaty of Fontainebleau was signed on April 11th, and Napoleon was forced into exile on the island of Elba off the Italian coast.

The Congress of Vienna

The Sixth Coalition succeeded where others had failed. Napoleon Bonaparte was no longer the dominant force in Europe. The guns fell silent, and Europe was at peace. However, the European powers faced a significant challenge. The Napoleonic Wars had been a period of conflict and enormous change. It was essential to establish a lasting peace and normalcy.

In Vienna, a conference of the major powers was held on November 1st, 1814. Klemens von Metternich chaired the conference. The Congress of Vienna impacted European politics for the next century.

The representatives were not interested in preserving any of the new liberties created by the Napoleonic Wars. They wanted to restore a sense of stability and peace to Europe. Essentially, the representatives were looking to achieve some form of *status quo ante.*

Five major European countries played deciding roles in the Vienna Congress.

- Austria was represented by Prince Klemens von Metternich.
- Russia was represented by Tsar Alexander I.
- Prussia was represented by Prince Karl August von Hardenberg.
- Great Britain was represented originally by Foreign Secretary Viscount Castlereagh and then later by the Duke of Wellington.

And the fifth? Well, it was France. Charles Maurice de Talleyrand-Périgord, the French foreign minister, represented France's interests at the congress. Despite being defeated, France played a prominent role in the Congress of Vienna thanks to Talleyrand's diplomatic skills.

Redrawing Europe

Napoleon had changed the borders of European countries, and now, the Congress of Vienna was going to redraw the map. It did not mean that the borders would be returned to their respective positions before the Napoleonic Wars. There was going to be a new Europe.

A new Kingdom of the Netherlands was one territorial change. This new state would include Belgium and serve as a buffer between Germany and France. Switzerland was recognized as a permanently neutral country, and it was another buffer state, this time between France and Italy.[90]

---

[90] Britannica, T. E. (2024, June 12). Congress of Vienna summary. Retrieved from Britannica.com: https://www.britannica.com/summary/Congress-of-Vienna.

The question of what to do with Germany was addressed. Reestablishing the Holy Roman Empire was out of the question; that empire was relegated to the history books. The Confederation of the Rhine also did not continue. The German Confederation, an association of thirty-nine German states, was created in its place. It would be under the control of Austria and was primarily established for mutual defense.

For whatever good intentions the Congress of Vienna had, the major players had agendas that included gaining territory. Austria received control of Lombardi and Venetia and land in the Balkans. Prussia received two-fifths of Saxony and extensive new territories in Westphalia and the left bank of the Rhine. Russia insisted on Polish territory, which caused some friction because Austria and Great Britain were concerned about Russia acquiring too much power. In the end, Russia received two-thirds of what was the Grand Duchy of Warsaw.[91]

In other land distributions, the German state of Hanover was enlarged, Piedmont gained possession of Genoa, the Papal States were restored to the pope, Denmark lost Norway to Sweden but got Lauenburg as compensation, and Swedish Pomerania was transferred to Prussia. Great Britain's colonial holdings increased, as the British received Malta, the Cape of Good Hope, and Ceylon. France was reduced to its original borders of 1792.[92]

Monarchies were restored. The Bourbons were placed back on the throne of France, and Ferdinand VII was once again the king of Spain. The sovereigns in Portugal, Naples, and Sardinia were restored. France lost territories taken during the French Revolution and the Napoleonic era, but it did not fare all that badly, primarily because of the efforts of Talleyrand.

The French foreign minister was a political chameleon. He was a Roman Catholic bishop before the French Revolution. He became an ardent revolutionary but later switched sides when Napoleon Bonaparte came to power. Napoleon had mixed feelings about the man but recognized Talleyrand's diplomatic skills. After Napoleon abdicated, the

---

[91] Schneid, F. C. (2024, June 12). Congress of Vienna. Retrieved from Encyclopedia.com: https://www.encyclopedia.com/history/encyclopedias-almanacs-transcripts-and-maps/congress-vienna.

[92] Britannica.com. (2024, June 12). Decisions of the Congress. Retrieved from Britannica.com: https://www.britannica.com/event/Congress-of-Vienna/Decisions-of-the-congress.

French king, Louis XVIII, made Talleyrand his foreign minister. Talleyrand's ability to play one side against the other during the Congress of Vienna prevented France from having to concede even more territory.[93]

Other issues, such as the free navigation of international rivers and a declaration advocating the abolition of the slave trade, were addressed at the Congress of Vienna. The most significant achievement was the understanding that all of this would create stability in Europe, with negotiations replacing armed conflict.

The Congress of Vienna was also a major social event. Delegates were invited to balls, concerts, and other forms of group entertainment where serious networking took place. Indeed, many agreements were reached on the ballroom floor before being decided at the conference.

The delegates could congratulate themselves on creating a new Europe that would hopefully be more peaceful and amicable. However, in March 1815, those diplomats received the shock of their lives.

Napoleon was back.

---

[93] Godechot, J. (2024, May 13). Charles-Maurice de Talleyrand, Prince de Benevent. Retrieved from Britannica.com: https://www.britannica.com/biography/Charles-Maurice-de-Talleyrand-prince-de-Benevent.

Chapter 11: The Hundred Days and Waterloo: Napoleon's Last Stand

Exile did not sit well with Napoleon. The former master of Europe was now confined to a small island off the coast of Italy. He had once commanded hundreds of thousands of men; now, he had to settle for a garrison of one thousand soldiers. Napoleon had to sit around and read accounts of what the Congress of Vienna was doing to change everything he had accomplished. He was more than just bored; he was angry. Finally, on February 26th, 1815, Napoleon Bonaparte escaped from Elba. He eluded the British ships that were supposed to guard him and landed in France on March 1st, 1815. He immediately set off for Paris.

His progress to the French capital was less of a journey than an imperial parade. Marshal Ney, who had pressured Napoleon to abdicate, was part of the Bourbon administration. He was sent to arrest Napoleon, but when Ney met his old commander, the marshal changed sides and joined ranks with Bonaparte. That kind of meeting was repeated constantly during the march as old veterans flocked to their emperor's banner.

Although their love of Napoleon was genuine, many French soldiers deserted the Bourbons because of their dissatisfaction with the new government. The army was reduced to peacetime levels, and approximately eleven thousand officers were cashiered with half pay.

Those who stayed in the army were forced to report to superiors who were reinstated to ranks they held before the revolution. This angered those men who had risen through the ranks due to their bravery and merit. Even Marshal Ney, now a Peer of France, was looked down on by the restored aristocrats because he was a commoner by birth. The veterans remembered the past victories and the prestige they enjoyed as part of the Grande Armée. They wanted a return to their former glory.

The Bourbon dynasty could not mount an offensive against this swell of popular sentiment, and Louis XVIII was forced to flee. The Congress of Vienna declared that Napoleon was an outlaw on March 13th, but that did not stop Bonaparte's advance. Napoleon entered Paris on March 20th, 1815.[94]

The Hundred Days

Ten of Napoleon's former marshals declared allegiance to him, and Napoleon created a government that would help him meet his objectives. He presented himself to the French public as a changed man who was uninterested in autocratic rule or any more conquests. One of his critics, Benjamin Constant, was asked to draw up a new constitution. Constant created a shared power government based on the British model. There would be a bicameral parliament that would work with the emperor. Censorship and the slave trade would be abolished. It was all part of a public relations campaign to convince people Napoleon was finished with empires, but very few believed him. There were even French who opposed him: Brittany and the Vendee regions revolted.

Napoleon had more significant problems to worry about than internal uprisings. His former enemies came together, ratifying a treaty of alliance on March 25th. The Seventh Coalition included Great Britain, Russia, Sweden, Austria, Prussia, and several smaller European states. Each great power was committed to providing 150,000 men, and, interestingly, they declared war not on France but on Napoleon himself.

There was a problem of coordination, though. The British and the Prussians were prepared to move immediately, but the Austrians and Russians were not. Therefore, it was decided that the invasion of France would take place on July 1st when the various armies were in the field.

---

[94] Nackaerts, B. (2024, June 13). The Lack of Opposition to the Execution of Marshal Ney. Retrieved from Napoleon-series.org: https://www.napoleon-series.org/research/biographies/c_executney.html.

Napoleon was not going to wait that long. He planned to take the battle to the enemy before they could be fully organized. However, he had to move quickly to raise a force to confront the coalition. Despite his earlier abdication, Napoleon was still a very popular figure, and he had the support of many French. Napoleon called for volunteers and reinstated the conscription. The wars had been brutal on France, but many young men were still willing to fight and perhaps share in the glory that Napoleon might achieve. The old military infrastructure Napoleon created was still intact, and the officers were ready to join the campaign. An important task was to reconstitute the Imperial Guard. These were the best soldiers of the Grande Armée and would be necessary in any upcoming battles. Like so many veterans, the guardsmen returned to service.

A combination of enthusiasm, loyalty, and recognition of imminent danger helped bring together a significant force. Although Napoleon could not raise an army comparable to what he had for the Austerlitz campaign or the Russian offensive, he gathered nearly 200,000 troops. The new recruits were rigorously trained, and the old timers were reoriented to military activity. Bonaparte was ready to fight within a matter of weeks.

Napoleon versus Wellington

It had all the makings of a major prize fight. Both Napoleon and the Duke of Wellington had achieved significant victories, and neither feared the other. It would be the French champion against the British champion; only one could win.

The Seventh Coalition began to organize its armies and prepare a strategy to defeat Napoleon. The Duke of Wellington, who was in Vienna attending the Congress of Vienna, was assigned the command of a coalition force that was forming in what is now Belgium. He immediately left the congress and headed toward Brussels to assume command. Once there, Wellington coordinated his activity with the other primary coalition commander, Marshal Gebhard Leberecht von Blücher, for the upcoming campaign.

Coordination and logistics planning required skillful diplomatic communications. Wellington maintained a good relationship with all the coalition forces. Just like Dwight D. Eisenhower in the preparation for D-Day, Wellington proved to be as much a diplomat as he was a general. That was critical because internal squabbling and misunderstanding had ruined earlier coalition efforts to defeat Napoleon. It was decided that the British and Prussian armies would defend the Low Countries. Once the Austrians and Russians were ready, those two armies would approach France from the east.

Napoleon knew that if he conducted a defensive campaign, it would be a repeat of 1814. He did not want that to happen, and the preemptive strike he decided to execute would enable him to defeat one coalition army and then turn and defeat the next. This strategy had worked before, and the French emperor believed he could force the Seventh Coalition into peace talks if he beat them on the field.

Striking at the coalition army in Belgium made perfect sense. The British and Prussians were dispersed and would have to scramble to organize as a unified force. The British did not have the best troops available, as the veterans of the Peninsular War were in North America, fighting the War of 1812 with the Americans.

Napoleon split his forces into three armies. One was stationed in southern France near the Alps to stop any Austrian advance from Italy. Another was placed on the border with Prussia to resist attacks from the east. Napoleon personally led the final group, the Armée du Nord (the Army of the North), into the Low Countries to confront Wellington and Blücher. Napoleon moved the Army of the North, which numbered 128,000 men, in relative secrecy and crossed into the Low Countries at Thuin near Charleroi on June 15th, 1815, and caught the Prussian army off guard.

The Armies Clash

By nightfall on June 15th, the French occupied Charleroi and had moved north, effectively creating a wedge between the Prussians and the British. Napoleon turned his attention toward the Prussians and, on June 16th, engaged them in a battle at Ligny. There, the Prussians were successfully outflanked and forced to retreat.

While Napoleon was dealing with the Prussians, the French left wing, under the command of Marshal Ney, engaged Wellington at Quatre Bras. Wellington was able to take a stronger stand, but Ney was able to keep the British from reinforcing the Prussians. Although the allies were able to maintain communication, Wellington could not move to aid the Prussians. Conversely, Ney was not able to assist Napoleon in attacking the Prussians.[95]

Wellington decided the best strategy was to retreat, so he moved his forces to the north. He finally stopped at a village named Waterloo, where he could set up a solid defensive position.

Napoleon followed the British retreat. Wishing to keep the Prussians and the British separate, Napoleon ordered Marshal Emmanuel de Grouchy to take thirty-three thousand men and pursue Blücher. De Grouchy's orders on the morning of June 17th were to keep close contact with the Prussians. More specific instructions came later that day, and de Grouchy was to move toward the town of Wavre. The French marshal was expected to keep the Prussians occupied and away from the battlefield where Napoleon would engage Wellington.

June 18th: The Day of Destiny

Waterloo would be the most significant battle fought on European soil for one hundred years. Napoleon had separated the Prussians and the British, and if he could prevent them from joining forces, there was a good chance he would win the next battle. Wellington had a strong defense, but that did not bother Bonaparte.

There was a storm the night before the battle, making the ground wet and muddy. Napoleon waited to allow the ground to dry so that his artillery would be more effective and his men could move more quickly. It is also possible that Napoleon was not feeling well. The French emperor needed some rest before commanding that day. Whatever the reasons, the delay allowed Wellington to prepare his defenses better and allowed the Prussians more time to advance toward the battlefield. The fighting commenced at 11:30 a.m.[96]

Two Farmhouses

There was a walled farmhouse named Hougoumont that was between the two armies. It was on the right flank of the British and protected the soldiers from a French attack. The battle began with a French attack on this farmhouse. Hougoumont would withstand seven attacks by

---

[95] Britishbattles.com. (2024, June 13). Battle of Quatre Bras. Retrieved from Britishbattles.com: https://www.britishbattles.com/napoleonic-wars/battle-of-quatre-bras/.

[96] Lentz, T. (2020, June). Bullet Point #35- How Did Napoleon Manage to Lose the Battle of Waterloo? Retrieved from Napoleon.org: https://www.napoleon.org/en/history-of-the-two-empires/articles/bullet-point-35-how-did-napoleon-manage-to-lose-the-battle-of-waterloo/.

Napoleon's infantry during the day. The coalition forces were able to hold onto the farmhouse, and the attacks on it diverted French soldiers who were needed elsewhere on the battlefield.[97]

Another farmhouse, La Haye Sainte, was at a central point directly in front of the main British lines. Napoleon ordered an infantry assault on the farmhouse at 1 p.m., but the coalition forces held it tenaciously. Once again, considerable forces were expended by the French to take La Haye Sainte. It finally fell in the late afternoon, but the French lost men and time in the assaults, and they could not afford to lose either.[98]

<u>Ney's Charge</u>

Late in the afternoon, around 4 p.m., Marshal Ney saw what he thought was a British retreat. The French marshal assembled the cavalry for a massive charge and led five thousand men in an assault. Unfortunately for Ney, those were not retreating British soldiers. They were wounded men being evacuated to the rear. Ney led the cavalry into British squares and artillery. Ney tried several times to break the squares, but he did not have infantry units backing them up, and half of the French cavalry reserve was lost in Ney's efforts.[99]

<u>Enter the Prussians</u>

De Grouchy did his best to keep the Prussians away from the Waterloo battlefield, but because he started moving late in the morning of June 17th, the Prussians had a head start. He was not sure where the Prussians were heading, and instead of following the advice of a staff officer to follow the sound of the guns, de Grouchy followed his original orders to head toward Wavre. He engaged the Prussian rearguard in that town, but the main Prussian troops moved directly to Waterloo.

The Prussians arrived on the eastern side of the battlefield at approximately 4:30 p.m. and began to engage the right flank of the French. By 6 p.m., the lion's share of the Prussian army was on the field at Waterloo and wearing down the French.

---

[97] Elmer, B. (2024, June 13). The Defense of Hougoumont. Retrieved from Napoleon-series.org: https://www.napoleon-series.org/military-info/battles/1815/waterloo/c_hougoumont.html.

[98] Simms, B. (2015, August 5). Holding the Farm at Waterloo. Retrieved from Historynet.com: https://www.historynet.com/holding-the-farm-at-waterloo/.

[99] Haskew, M. (2024, June 13). Marshal Ney and His Biggest Mistake at the Battle of Waterloo. Retrieved from Warfarehistorynetwork.com: https://warfarehistorynetwork.com/marshal-ney-and-his-biggest-mistake-at-the-battle-of-waterloo/.

The Advance of the Guard

Napoleon repeatedly tried to break through Wellington's lines but was unsuccessful. The Prussian army was now engaged, and the situation became desperate for the French. At around 7:30 p.m., Napoleon ordered the Imperial Guard to advance, hoping this one last move would break the enemy lines.

The Imperial Guard could not break through despite all their efforts. The British held, and the Imperial Guard was finally forced to retreat. That was the turning point of the battle. The French army, upon seeing the retreat of the Imperial Guard, began to panic, and the French soldiers retreated in a disorganized fashion. Napoleon realized the battle was lost and left the battlefield around 8:30 p.m. His army was in retreat, and he needed to reorganize what was left. He probably knew that it was all over for him.

Napoleon's Fate

Napoleon abdicated for a second time on June 22nd, 1815. He wanted to seek asylum in Great Britain but was turned down immediately in favor of having him exiled. An interesting question is why the former emperor was not executed. That would have solved the question of what to do with him permanently.

The answer is complex and reflects the political realities of the time. There were still many people devoted to Napoleon and turning him into a martyr would upset the political situation in Europe, which was already fragile. Moreover, although the monarchs hated Napoleon, they did not want to set a precedent where a deposed ruler would be executed. Political stability was the order of the day, and sending Napoleon into exile removed him from the European stage and put him in a place where he could be closely watched.

Napoleon's days of influencing European policy were over. He was exiled to the island of Saint Helena, a spit of land in the Atlantic Ocean one thousand miles from Europe. Napoleon lived the rest of his life there. He passed away on May 5th, 1821. There is a legend that the former French emperor was gradually poisoned during his exile, but to this day, there is no corroboration of what the poison was or who was the poisoner.

The Second Treaty of Paris was signed on November 20th, 1815 (the first one was signed in 1814) and had firm stipulations. France had to pay an indemnity of seven hundred million francs, and its borders were reduced to those that existed on January 1ˢᵗ, 1790. All the territory it had gained in the French Revolution was lost. France would be required to cover the expenses of any additional fortifications built by neighboring coalition countries, and to add insult to injury, 150,000 foreign troops would occupy France in designated zones. These would stay there until 1818 when they were removed. The allies wanted stability in Europe, and the terms would prevent France from becoming a problem in the foreseeable future.

An interesting development in the Congress of Vienna was the Holy Alliance. This was an idea that Tsar Alexander promoted. His intention was to promote Christian principles in nations' affairs. It was formed in Paris on September 26th, 1815, while negotiations for the Second Treaty of Paris were finalized. The primary advocates were Alexander of Russia, Francis I of Austria, and Frederick William III of Prussia. The irony is that they were promoting Christian principles, and one nation was Roman Catholic, one was Russian Orthodox, and one was Protestant.

The Holy Alliance was more an enforcer than a moral guide. It was there to uphold the new conservatism regimes, and many liberals suspected that the alliance would be used to suppress liberal tendencies. The Holy Alliance did stifle dissent, but it was also an example of cooperative effort that gradually became the norm for European countries in the 19th century.[100]

The Demise of the Empire

Not one event or reason brought an end to Napoleon's empire. The man was a military genius, but he made mistakes. Some were easy to correct, but others created situations that ultimately produced negative consequences. Let's take a moment to look at some of his more critical missteps.

- The Continental System

    It was a disaster, pure and simple. Napoleon wanted to choke Great Britain economically but did not appreciate that British trade was global. A loss of trade in one country could be compensated for by additional commerce in the Americas or India. Capitalism permitted Great Britain to rebound from the

---

[100] Britannica, T. E. (2024, June 13). Holy Alliance. Retrieved from Britannica.com: https://www.britannica.com/topic/Holy-Alliance.

embargo.

The Continental System created difficulties and encouraged smuggling. The nations forced to be a part of it faced an economic downturn, and that included France.

France's international image was also hurt. Enforcing the Continental System made Napoleon look more authoritarian than ever before. He was no longer the great liberator but the oppressive enforcer. The animosity and resentment caused by the Continental System would haunt him a few years later.

- The Russian Campaign

This was the worst military decision Napoleon ever made. The logistics alone were enough to defeat any army, but Napoleon's stubborn ego was a big reason for the defeat. He was smart enough to know that the Russians were deliberately retreating in front of him, drawing the Grande Armée deeper and deeper into Russia. He could have stopped and waited for the Russians to come to him, but Moscow was an obsessive objective for him. France never fully recovered from the losses.

- The Peninsular War

It was an open wound that bled France's treasury. Napoleon was required to station thousands of troops in the Iberian Peninsula, regiments he could have used elsewhere. British persistence and guerrilla attacks created significant problems the French emperor could not solve.

- The Cost of War

The French were at war almost continuously in the first fifteen years of the 19th century. It put an enormous strain on the French economy, but it also affected France's allies and subjugated territories. France was unable to match Great Britain when it came to raising money. Napoleon had to rely on increasing taxes, tribute from the empire and the satellite states, and the indemnities imposed on defeated nations.

- Poor Quality of Leadership

Napoleon was a military genius, but his governing style was more autocratic than egalitarian. He was prone to rule by decrees and not compromise. Placing his family members on various thrones was not a good idea. His siblings were nowhere near as competent as he was. His dream of Bonaparte dynasties all over Europe quickly collapsed when he started to lose.

- Nationalism

    Napoleon spread the ideals of nationalism by crippling old empires. The demise of the Holy Roman Empire led to the creation of the Confederation of the Rhine, which meant that large German states took the place of autonomous cities. Italy was more unified than ever before; Bonaparte gets the credit for that.

    However, with nationalism came the idea of self-determination. Countries began to turn against French domination, and nationalist movements that resisted French hegemony started to rise.

- Military Reforms

    It required several disastrous military campaigns, but Napoleon's enemies finally understood they could not hope to beat the French emperor unless serious military reforms were enacted. Prussia and Austria, in particular, made significant changes in military management. Several coalitions tried and failed to beat Napoleon, but the Sixth Coalition finally got it right. Members of the alliance put their differences aside temporarily and united in a common purpose to defeat France. The Battle of Leipzig demonstrated what the European powers could do once they were united in achieving their goal.

The era of the Napoleonic Wars was over. Conflicts and wars would still be fought on the European continent, but these actions did not involve all the nations. A conservative frame of mind became the dominant mood and would be so for several decades. The Napoleonic era was finished; the Age of Metternich began.

Conclusion

The Napoleonic Wars were an epoch of change, often accompanied by violence. Yet, as the years unfolded, Europe's resilience shone through, transforming the continent. Europe emerged as a new entity, forever altered from its prewar state, a testament to its ability to adapt and evolve.

The Age of Metternich, spearheaded by the influential Prince Metternich, was a significant attempt to restore Europe to a conservative mindset. While it succeeded initially, the revolutionary ideas that had been implemented in the early 19th century were never entirely abandoned. The significant convulsion that Europe experienced in 1848 marked a profound shift from conservatism to liberalism, a turning point in history.

After the Napoleonic Wars, Europe underwent a societal shift. The societies of Europe, having tasted a degree of freedom that had been absent in the 18th century, were not willing to revert to the Ancien Régime. Europe was now a new world of nations, with Italy and Germany no longer mere geographical expressions. This societal transformation was a direct result of the Napoleonic Wars.

Europe needed to go through that period of turmoil. Some changes were so dramatic that military action was the only way to guarantee these innovations would be part of the social and political order. Millions died, but the changes were made, and some of the reforms, such as the Napoleonic Code, are still significant influences.

The Napoleonic Wars were not just a chaotic period of change but also a defining moment in European history. The break from tradition was not peaceful, but it was permanent. Today, Europe's social, political, and geographical landscape traces its roots back to that epoch, a testament to the profound and lasting impact of this historical era.

If you enjoyed this book, a review on Amazon would be greatly appreciated because it would mean a lot to hear from you.

To leave a review:
1. Open your camera app.
2. Point your mobile device at the QR code.
3. The review page will appear in your web browser.

Thanks for your support!

Here's another book by Enthralling History
that you might like

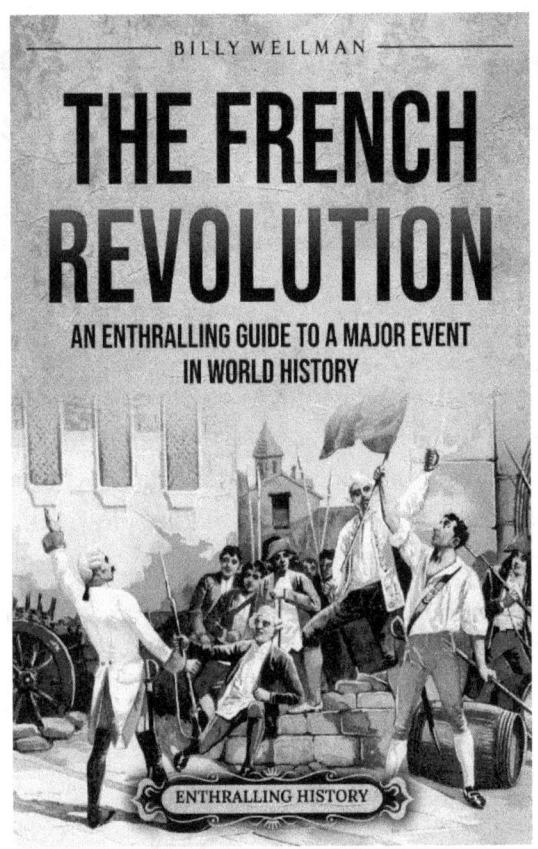

Free limited time bonus

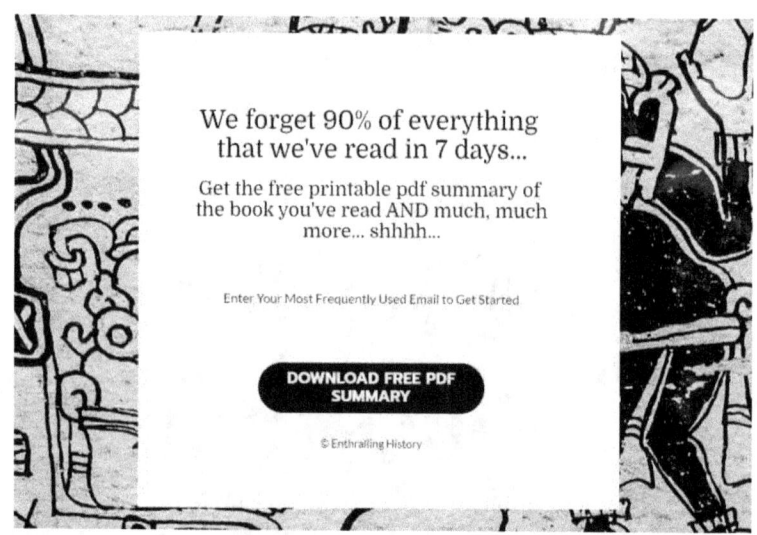

Stop for a moment. We have a free bonus set up for you. The problem is this: we forget 90% of everything that we read after 7 days. Crazy fact, right? Here's the solution: we've created a printable, 1-page pdf summary for this book that you're reading now. All you have to do to get your free pdf summary is to go to the following website: https://livetolearn.lpages.co/enthrallinghistory/

Or, Scan the QR code!

Once you do, it will be intuitive. Enjoy, and thank you!

Bibliography

Anne S. K. Brown Military Collection. (2024, June 4). Napoleonic Satires. Retrieved from library.brown.edu: https://library.brown.edu/cds/napoleon/time2.html.

Anonymous. (2024, June 8). War of the Fourth Coalition. Retrieved from Resources.saylor.org: https://resources.saylor.org/wwwresources/archived/site/wp-content/uploads/2011/05/War-of-the-Fourth-coalition.pdf.

Bainbridge, S. (2016, June 2). Romanticism and War. Retrieved from Oxford Academic: https://academic.oup.com/edited-volume/43514/chapter/364255284?login=false.

Britannica, E. o. (2024, May 14). Battle of Ulm. Retrieved from Britannica.com: https://www.britannica.com/event/Battle-of-Ulm.

Britannica, E. o. (2024, May 18). Napoleonic Code. Retrieved from Britannica.com: https://www.britannica.com/topic/Napoleonic-Code.

Britannica, E. o. (2024, May 14). Siege of Toulon. Retrieved from Britannica.com: https://www.britannica.com/event/Siege-of-Toulon.

Britannica, T. E. (2024, May 24). Banque de France. Retrieved from Britannica.com: https://www.britannica.com/money/Banque-de-France.

Britannica, T. E. (2024, May 14). Battle of Dresden. Retrieved from Britannica.com: https://www.britannica.com/event/Battle-of-Dresden.

Britannica, T. E. (2024, June 12). Congress of Vienna Summary. Retrieved from Britannica.com: https://www.britannica.com/summary/Congress-of-Vienna.

Britannica, T. E. (2024, May 23). Haitian Revolution. Retrieved from Britannica.com: https://www.britannica.com/topic/Haitian-Revolution.

Britannica, T. E. (2024, June 13). Holy Alliance. Retrieved from Britannica.com: https://www.britannica.com/topic/Holy-Alliance.

Britannica, T. E. (2024, May 9). Manuel de Godoy. Retrieved from Britannica.com: https://www.britannica.com/biography/Manuel-de-Godoy#ref112973

Britannica, T. E. (2024, April 30). Peninsular War. Retrieved from Britannica.com: https://www.britannica.com/event/Peninsular-War.

Britannica, T. E. (2024, June 11). Treaty of Schonbrunn. Retrieved from Britannica.com: https://www.britannica.com/event/Treaty-of-Schonbrunn.

Britannica.com. (2024, June 12). Decisions of the Congress. Retrieved from Britannica.com: https://www.britannica.com/event/Congress-of-Vienna/Decisions-of-the-congress.

Britannica.com. (2024, June 4). End of the Holy Roman Empire. Retrieved from Britannica.com: https://www.britannica.com/place/Germany/End-of-the-Holy-Roman-Empire

Britannica.com. (2024, May 28). Great Britan, France, and the Neutrals, 1800-1802. Retrieved from Britannica.com: https://www.britannica.com/event/Napoleonic-Wars/Great-Britain-France-and-the-neutrals-1800-02

Britannica.com. (2024, May 14). The Austrian Attempt at Mediation. Retrieved from Britannica.com: https://www.britannica.com/event/Napoleonic-Wars/The-Austrian-attempt-at-mediation

Britishbattles.com. (2024, June 13). Battle of Quatre Bras. Retrieved from Britishbattles.com: https://www.britishbattles.com/napoleonic-wars/battle-of-quatre-bras/.

Burkholder, S. H. (2024, June 10). Treaty of Fontainebleau (1807). Retrieved from Encyclopedia.com: https://www.encyclopedia.com/humanities/encyclopedias-almanacs-transcripts-and-maps/fontainebleau-treaty-1807.

Cheikh, M. (2020, September 24). Were Metternich's Peace Ouvertures in 1813 Genuine? Retrieved from Thenapoleonicwars.net: https://www.thenapoleonicwars.net/forum/napoleon/were-metternich-s-peace-ouvertures-in-1813-genuine.

Colley, L. J. (2024, June 8). The Napoleonic Wars. Retrieved from Britannica.com: https://www.britannica.com/place/United-Kingdom/The-Napoleonic-Wars.

Collinson, A. (2015, May 11). In Literature and Song: The Legacy of the Napoleonic Wars. Retrieved from Ageofrevolution.org: https://ageofrevolution.org/in-literature-and-song-the-legacy-of-the-napoleonic-wars/.

Coppa, F. J. (2018, May 18). Concordat of 1801. Retrieved from Encyclopedia.com: https://www.encyclopedia.com/philosophy-and-religion/christianity/roman-catholic-and-orthodox-churches-councils-and-treaties/concordat-1801.

DailyHistory.org. (2024, May 26). Why Has the French Civil Code Had a Lasting Influence on Contemporary European Law. Retrieved from DailyHistory.org: https://www.dailyhistory.org/Why_has_the_French_Civil_Code_had_a_lasting_influence_on_contemporary_European_law.

DetailedPedia.com. (2024, June 11). Battle of Smolensk (1812). Retrieved from Detailedpedia.com: https://www.detailedpedia.com/wiki-Battle_of_Smolensk_%281812%29.

DetailedPedia.com. (2024, May 26). Napoleonic Code. Retrieved from DetailedPedia.com: https://www.detailedpedia.com/wiki-Napoleonic_Code.

Editors, H. (2023, April 24). Napoleon Bonaparte. Retrieved from History.com: https://www.history.com/topics/european-history/napoleon.

Elmer, B. (2024, June 13). The Defense of Hougoumont. Retrieved from Napoleon-series.org: https://www.napoleon-series.org/military-info/battles/1815/waterloo/c_hougoumont.html.

Emerson Kent.com. (2024, May 25). Taxation in Pre-Revolutionary France. Retrieved from Emersonkent.com: http://www.emersonkent.com/history_dictionary/taxation_in_pre_revolutionary_france.htm.

Encyclopedia.com. (2018, May 23). Battle of Trafalgar. Retrieved from Encyclopedia.com: https://www.encyclopedia.com/history/modern-europe/wars-and-battles/battle-trafalgar.

Ernest McNeil Eller, R. L. (2024, June 4). Ships of the Line. Retrieved from Britannica.com: https://www.britannica.com/technology/naval-ship/Ship-of-the-line.

Foscolo, U. (2024, June 11). Ugo Foscolo-Opere Omnia. Retrieved from Foscolo.letteraturaoperaomnia.org: https://foscolo.letteraturaoperaomnia.org/foscolo_dei_sepolcri.html.

Franciscogoya.com. (2024, June 10). The Disaster of War, 1810-1820 by Francisco Goya. Retrieved from Franciscogoya.com: https://www.franciscogoya.com/disasters-of-war.jsp.

Frithowulf, H. (2024, February 29). Battle of Wagram: Napoleon's Masterstroke. Retrieved from Malevus.com: https://malevus.com/battle-of-wagram/.

Globallytaught.com. (2024, May 26). Education Systems Around the World: A Look at 4 Top School Systems. Retrieved from Globallytaught.com:

https://globallytaught.com/blog/education-systems-around-the-world/.

Godechot, J. (2024, May 13). Charles-Maurice de Talleyrand, Prince de Benevent. Retrieved from Britannica.com: https://www.britannica.com/biography/Charles-Maurice-de-Talleyrand-prince-de-Benevent.

Green, J. (2002, April). Michel Ney's Retreat. Retrieved from Warfarenetwork.com: https://warfarehistorynetwork.com/article/michel-neys-retreat/.

Green, J. (2004, April). Napoleon Bonaparte's "Roland": Marshal Jean Lannes. Retrieved from Warfarehistorynetwork.com: https://warfarehistorynetwork.com/article/napoleon-bonapartes-roland-marshal-jean-lannes/.

Haskew, M. (2024, June 13). Marshal Ney and His Biggest Mistake at the Battle of Waterloo. Retrieved from Warfarehistorynetwork.com: https://warfarehistorynetwork.com/marshal-ney-and-his-biggest-mistake-at-the-battle-of-waterloo/.

Hickman, K. (2015, March 10). Napoleonic Wars: Battle of Aspern-Essling. Retrieved from Thoughtco.com: https://www.thoughtco.com/napoleonic-battle-of-aspern-essling-2361108.

Hickman, K. (2019, September 4). French Revolutionary Wars: Battle of Valmy. Retrieved from ThoughtCo.: https://www.thoughtco.com/french-revolution-battle-of-valmy-2361106.

Hickman, K. (2020, January 2). Napoleonic Wars: Marshall Jean-Baptiste Bernadotte. Retrieved from ThoughtCo.com: https://www.thoughtco.com/napoleonic-wars-marshal-jean-baptiste-bernadotte-2360137.

Hicks, P. (2024, June 4). The Royal Navy, 1793-1802. Retrieved from Napoleon.org: https://www.napoleon.org/en/history-of-the-two-empires/articles/the-british-navy-1793-1802/.

History Skills. (2024, June 10). What Was Napoleon's Revolutionary Continental System and How Did It Shape Modern Europe. Retrieved from Historyskills.com: https://www.historyskills.com/classroom/modern-history/continental-system/.

Historyskills.com. (2024, June 11). Napoleon's Catastrophic Invasion of Russia: A Military Miscalculation of Epic Proportions. Retrieved from Historyskills.com: https://www.historyskills.com/classroom/modern-history/napoleon-s-russian-invasion/.

Jacques Godechot, E. P. (2024, April 30). Arthur Wellesley, 1st Duke of Wellington. Retrieved from Britannica.com:

https://www.britannica.com/biography/Arthur-Wellesley-1st-Duke-of-Wellington.

Jensen, N. D. (2024, May 25). Organization of French Revolutionary Armies 1791-1801. Retrieved from French Empire.net: https://www.frenchempire.net/articles/armies/.

Keene, R. (2024, June 10). Napoleon and Goethe: Touchstone of Genius. Retrieved from Thearticle.com: https://www.thearticle.com/napoleon-and-goethe-touchstone-of-genius.

Lee, A. (2018, March 3). Beethoven and Napoleon. Retrieved from Historytoday.com: https://www.historytoday.com/archive/music-time/beethoven-and-napoleon.

Lentz, T. (2020, June). Bullet Point #35- How Did Napoleon Manage to Lose the Battle of Waterloo? Retrieved from Napoleon.org: https://www.napoleon.org/en/history-of-the-two-empires/articles/bullet-point-35-how-did-napoleon-manage-to-lose-the-battle-of-waterloo/.

Lord Byron. The Works of Lord Byron Vol. 2. https://genius.com/Lord-byron-the-works-of-lord-byron-vol-2-to-inez-annotated.

Marino Berengo, C. M. (2024, June 4). Italy-The Napoleonic Empire 1804-14. Retrieved from Britannica.com: https://www.britannica.com/place/Italy/The-acquisition-of-Venetia-and-Rome.

Mark, H. W. (2022, March 7). The Three Estates of Pre-Revolutionary France. Retrieved from World History Encyclopedia: https://www.worldhistory.org/article/1960/the-three-estates-of-pre-revolutionary-france/.

Mark, H. W. (2023, July 24). Battle of Eylau. Retrieved from World History Encyclopedia: https://www.worldhistory.org/article/2258/battle-of-eylau/.

Mark, H. W. (2023, July 25). Battle of Friedland. Retrieved from World History Encyclopedia: https://www.worldhistory.org/article/2259/battle-of-friedland/.

Mark, H. W. (2023, June 19). Battle of Jena-Auerstedt. Retrieved from World History Encyclopedia: https://www.worldhistory.org/article/2256/battle-of-jena-auerstedt/.

Mark, H. W. (2023, August 16). Battle of Wagram. Retrieved from World History: https://www.worldhistory.org/article/2267/battle-of-wagram/

Mark, H. W. (2023, August 3). Continental System. Retrieved from World History Encyclopedia.com: https://www.worldhistory.org/Continental_System/.

Mark, H. W. (2023, July 6). Coronation of Napoleon I. Retrieved from World History Encyclopedia.com: https://www.worldhistory.org/article/2251/coronation-of-napoleon-i/.

Mark, H. W. (2023, October 3). Hundred Days. Retrieved from World History Encyclopedia: https://www.worldhistory.org/Hundred_Days/

Mark, H. W. (2023, August 7). Peninsular War. Retrieved from World History Encyclopedia: https://www.worldhistory.org/Peninsular_War/.

Mark, H. W. (2023, July 10). Ulm Campaign. Retrieved from World History Encyclopedia: https://www.worldhistory.org/article/2249/ulm-campaign/.

Mark, H. W. (2023, July 28). War of the Fourth Coalition. Retrieved from World History Encyclopedia: https://www.worldhistory.org/War_of_the_Fourth_Coalition/.

Mark, H. W. (2023, September 4). War of the Sixth Coalition. Retrieved from World History Encyclopedia: https://www.worldhistory.org/War_of_the_Sixth_Coalition/.

Mark, H. W. (2023, July 18). War of the Third Coalition. Retrieved from World History Encyclopedia: https://www.worldhistory.org/War_of_the_Third_Coalition/.

Musee Goya Castres. (2024, June 10). Goya-Picasso: A Cross-View. Retrieved from museegoya.fr: https://www.museegoya.fr/en/goya-in-piccaso-s-eye.

Nackaerts, B. (2024, June 13). The Lack of Opposition to the Execution of Marshal Ney. Retrieved from Napoleon-series.org: https://www.napoleon-series.org/research/biographies/c_executeney.html.

Napoleon & Empire. (2024, May 14). Battle of Eylau. Retrieved from Napoleon &Empire.net: https://www.napoleon-empire.net/en/battles/eylau.php.

Napoleonguide.com. (2024, May 25). Lazare Carnot. Retrieved from Napoleonguide.com: https://www.napoleonguide.com/carnot.htm.

Napoleon.org. (2010, March). The Marriage of Napoleon I and Marie-Louise of Austria. Retrieved from Napoleon.org: https://www.napoleon.org/en/history-of-the-two-empires/timelines/the-marriage-of-napoleon-i-and-marie-louise-of-austria/.

Napoleon.org. (2020, December). Napoleon I and His Family. Retrieved from Napoleon.org: https://www.napoleon.org/en/young-historians/napodoc/napoleon-i-and-his-family/.

Napoleon.org. (2024, May 28). Louis-Alexandre Berthier. Retrieved from Napoleon.org: https://www.napoleon.org/en/history-of-the-two-empires/biographies/berthier-louis-alexandre/.

Napoleon.org. (2024, June 11). Napoleon's Russian Campaign: The Retreat. Retrieved from Napoleon.org: https://www.napoleon.org/en/history-of-the-two-empires/timelines/napoleons-russian-campaign-the-retreat/.

Napoleonistyka.atspace.com. (2024, May 28). Russian Army of the Napoleonic Wars. Retrieved from Napoleonistyka.atspace.com:

Napoleonistyka.atspace.com.

National Army Museum. (2024, June 10). Peninsular War. Retrieved from Nam.ac.uk: https://www.nam.ac.uk/explore/peninsular-war.

New World Encyclopedia. (2024, June 4). Battle of Austerlitz. Retrieved from New World Encyclopedia.org: https://www.newworldencyclopedia.org/entry/Battle_of_Austerlitz.

New World Encyclopedia. (2024, June 11). French Invasion of Russia. Retrieved from New World Encyclopedia.com: https://www.newworldencyclopedia.org/entry/French_invasion_of_Russia#Retreat_and_losses.

Pisa, J. d. (2011, October 5). Napoleon's Nightmare: Guerilla Warfare in Spain (1808-1814). Retrieved from Smallwarsjournal.com: https://smallwarsjournal.com/jrnl/art/napoleon%c2%b4s-nightmare-guerrilla-warfare-in-spain-1808-1814.

Pock, T. (2024, June 4). Battles of Cape St. Vincent and the Nile. Retrieved from Britannica.com: https://www.britannica.com/biography/Horatio-Nelson/Battles-of-Cape-St-Vincent-and-the-Nile.

Pocock, T. (2024, June 4). Horatio Nelson at Trafalgar. Retrieved from Britannica.com: https://www.britannica.com/biography/Horatio-Nelson/Victory-at-Trafalgar.

Powerplace.org. (2023, July 28). Top 51 Timeless Sun Tzu Quotes: Mastering Strategy and Leadership. Retrieved from Powerplace.org: https://powerplace.org/blogs/quotes/mastering-strategy-and-leadership-unveiling-51-timeless-sun-tzu-quotes.

Royal Navy. (2024, June 4). Trafalgar Day. Retrieved from Royalnavy.mod.uk: https://www.royalnavy.mod.uk/news-and-latest-activity/events/national/171021-trafalgar-day.

Savoie, P. (2024, May 26). Lycée. Retrieved from Faqs.org: http://www.faqs.org/childhood/Ke-Me/Lyc-e.html.

Schneid, F. C. (2024, June 12). Congress of Vienna. Retrieved from Encyclopedia.com: https://www.encyclopedia.com/history/encyclopedias-almanacs-transcripts-and-maps/congress-vienna.

Setterfield, R. (2019, November 18). Horatio Nelson: From Frail Boy to National Hero. Retrieved from Onthisday.com: https://www.onthisday.com/articles/horatio-nelson-from-frail-boy-to-national-hero.

Simms, B. (2015, August 5). Holding the Farm at Waterloo. Retrieved from Historynet.com: https://www.historynet.com/holding-the-farm-at-waterloo/.

Sparknotes.com. (2024, May 25). The French Revolution (1789-1799). Retrieved from Sparknotes.com:

https://www.sparknotes.com/history/european/frenchrev/section1/.

The Clark. (2024, June 10). David & Napoleon. Retrieved from Clarkart.edu: https://www.clarkart.edu/microsites/jacques-louis-david/david-napoleon.

The Open University. (2024, June 10). 3 Gros and the Napoleonic Propaganda Machine. Retrieved from Open.edu: https://www.open.edu/openlearn/history-the-arts/history-art/napoleonic-paintings/content-section-3.1.

Thenapoleonicwars.net. (2024, June 11). Napoleon's Invasion of Russia. Retrieved from Thenapoleonicwars.net: https://www.thenapoleonicwars.net/invasion-of-russia.

Wesson, M. J. (2024, May 28). The Development of the Corps d'armée and Its Impact on Napoleonic Warfare. Retrieved from The Napoleon Series: https://www.napoleon-series.org/military-info/organization/c_armycorps.html.

Williamson, M. (2016, August 5). French Napoleonic Artillery in Action. Retrieved from Weapons and Warfare: https://weaponsandwarfare.com/2016/08/06/french-napoleonic-artillery-in-action/.

Wordsworth, W. (2024, June 19). Elegias Stanzas Suggested by a Picture of Peele Castle in a Storm, Painted by Sir George Beaumont. Retrieved from Poetryfoundation.org: https://www.poetryfoundation.org/poems/45516/elegiac-stanzas-suggested-by-a-picture-of-peele-castle-in-a-storm-painted-by-sir-george-beaumont.

Image Sources

[i] https://commons.wikimedia.org/wiki/File:Vig%C3%A9e-Lebrun,_Elisabeth-Louise_-_Charles-Alexandre_de_Calonne_(1734-1802)_-_Google_Art_Project.jpg

[ii] https://commons.wikimedia.org/wiki/File:Valmy_Battle_painting.jpg

[iii] https://commons.wikimedia.org/wiki/File:13Vend%C3%A9miaire.jpg

[iv] https://commons.wikimedia.org/wiki/File:Pappenheim_Curassiers.PNG

[v] https://commons.wikimedia.org/wiki/File:David_-_Napoleon_crossing_the_Alps_-_Malmaison2.jpg

[vi] https://commons.wikimedia.org/wiki/File:Murat2.jpg

[vii] *Clem le Nem, CC0, via Wikimedia Commons;*
https://commons.wikimedia.org/wiki/File:France_September_1812_prussia_occupied2.png

[viii] https://commons.wikimedia.org/wiki/File:Jacques-Louis_David_-_The_Emperor_Napoleon_in_His_Study_at_the_Tuileries_-_Google_Art_Project.jpg

[ix] https://commons.wikimedia.org/wiki/File:Boutigny-Surrender_at_Ulm.jpg

[x] https://commons.wikimedia.org/wiki/File:HoratioNelson1.jpg

[xi] https://commons.wikimedia.org/wiki/File:Treaties_of_Tilsit_miniature_(France,_1810s)_side_A.jpg

[xii] https://commons.wikimedia.org/wiki/File:Manuel_de_Godoy,_por_Francisco_Bayeu_(Real_Academia_de_Bellas_Artes_de_San_Fernando).jpg

[xiii] https://commons.wikimedia.org/wiki/File:Joseph-Bonaparte.jpg

[xiv] https://commons.wikimedia.org/wiki/File:Sir_Arthur_Wellesley,_1st_Duke_of_Wellington.png

[xv] https://commons.wikimedia.org/wiki/File:Eroica_Beethoven_title.jpg

[xvi] https://commons.wikimedia.org/wiki/File:Jacques-Louis_David_-_The_Coronation_of_Napoleon_(1805-1807).jpg

[xvii] https://commons.wikimedia.org/wiki/File:El_dos_de_mayo_de_1808_en_Madrid.jpg
[xviii] https://commons.wikimedia.org/wiki/File:Prado_-_Los_Desastres_de_la_Guerra_-_No._03_-_Lo_mismo.jpg
[xix] https://commons.wikimedia.org/wiki/File:Marie_Louise_von_%C3%96sterreich_Napoleon_Zweite.jpg
[xx] https://commons.wikimedia.org/wiki/File:Battle_of_Borodino_1812.png
[xxi] https://commons.wikimedia.org/wiki/File:Night_Bivouac_of_Great_Army.jpg
[xxii] https://commons.wikimedia.org/wiki/File:Carl_XIV_John_of_Sweden_%26_Norway_c_1840.jpg
[xxiii] https://commons.wikimedia.org/wiki/File:MoshkovVI_SrazhLeypcigomGRM.jpg

www.ingramcontent.com/pod-product-compliance
Lightning Source LLC
Chambersburg PA
CBHW070334010526
44107CB00004B/508